Origami
Sourcebook

Origami Sourcebook

Beautiful Projects and Mythical Characters, Step-by-Step

Jay Ansill

Photographs by Mark Hill

GLOUCESTER MASSACHUSETTS

QUARRY BOOKS

Pages 6–159 ©Running Heads
Pages 160–171 ©Quarry Books

Published by Quarry Books, an imprint of
Rockport Publishers, Inc.
33 Commercial Street
Gloucester, Massachusetts 01930-5089
Telephone: (978) 282-9590
Fax: (978) 283-2742
www.rockpub.com

Library of Congress Cataloging-in-Publication data available

ISBN 1-59253-065-6

10 9 8 7 6 5 4 3 2 1

Layout and production: Leslie Haimes
Cover design: Jean Debenedictis

Grateful acknowledgment is given to Michael G. LaFosse for his work from *Make It with Paper: Paper Animals* on pages 162–167, and also for his work from *Make It with Paper: Paper Boxes* on pages 168–173.

Printed in Singapore

Contents

The Basics

Paper Choices

Most art supply stores and hobby shops carry packaged origami paper. This comes in precut squares of various sizes and is colored on one side and white on the other. Most models are well suited to this kind of paper, although brands vary in quality and some papers are not cut accurately. Accurate size is an extremely important requirement because if the dimensions are wrong, folding accurately is impossible and the finished model will look sloppy.

Often foil paper can be found. This is usually silver or gold on one side and white on the other. Although this kind of paper retains folds well, any crease or wrinkle is permanent, so certain models can look sloppy if multiple folds are used to achieve the final result.

Since many of the models in this book are decorative in nature, it is a good idea to use a variety of papers to accent this feature. A great place to start the search for nice paper is the giftwrap department of a stationer's shop. Wrapping paper comes in hundreds of colors, textures, and patterns, and is generally easy to fold. Wallpaper can provide some interesting results, but it is important to make sure that it doesn't crack when folded. Practically anything can work. Try maps, pages from magazines and catalogues, flyers, and the like. I've even had luck folding music paper.

Sometimes it is interesting to give a model an added dimension. Two techniques that have been developed to make this possible are wet folding and tissue foil. Wet folding requires a sheet of paper that is a bit absorbent (calligraphy parchment works well), a spray bottle or bowl of water, and a cloth. During the folding process, the paper is kept slightly damp so that it can be sculpted, and the finished piece becomes stiff when dried.

Tissue foil is made by attaching a piece of tissue paper to both sides of a piece of aluminum foil with spray adhesive. This result is paper that is extremely flexible with an interesting texture. It can be sculpted to give extra character to animals. This kind of paper is great for making very complex models.

The fact that origami demands so few tools is one of the most appealing characteristics of the art form. All that is really needed is a sheet of paper. Often, the most striking result comes from an unlikely source. Be imaginative, resourceful, and adventurous, and the charm, beauty, and sheer enjoyment of origami will be revealed.

Basic Folds, Symbols, and Bases

An illustrative system of lines, dots, dashes, and arrows has been devised to make the diagrams easier to understand. Most origami books use these symbols, which constitute an international visual language. Although the diagrams that follow are self-explanatory, keep in mind the following principles:

- Arrows indicate the direction of a fold.
- Dots and dashes are used to indicate the folds themselves.
- Dashes alone indicate a concave crease, or valley fold.
- Dots alternating with dashes indicate a convex crease, or mountain fold; in this case, the paper is over.
- Throughout the book, diagrams are shaded to indicate the colored side of the paper should be facing outward.

Also included in this section are traditional Japanese bases. These are named for ancient models that use them as a starting point. Hundreds of contemporary models are folder from these bases. Like musical scales, they are the stepping stones to creativity and innovation. In many of the introductions to the models, the text will refer to one of these folds or bases as a starting point. Simply turn to this page to find the fold or base, and then resume with the step-by-step directions provided for the particular model.

Valley fold—fold forward

Mountain fold—fold behind

Existing fold or crease

X-ray view or guidelines

Fold in direction of arrow

Fold behind

Unfold

Fold and unfold

Push in, sink, squash, or reverse fold

Turn model over

Pleat fold
(combination of mountain and valley folds)

Repeat behind; 2 lines indicate twice

Enlarged view

Preliminary Fold

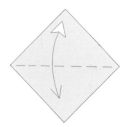

1. Fold and unfold.

2. Fold and unfold.

3. Turn over.

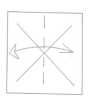

4. Fold and unfold.

5.

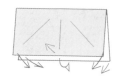

6a. Bring corners together.

6b.

1–6b.

7. Completed Preliminary Fold.

Petal Fold

1. Begin with Preliminary Fold

2.

3. Unfold.

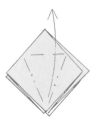

4a. Lift flap as far as it will go.

4b.

4c.

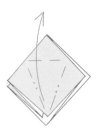

1–4c.

5. Completed Petal Fold.

Bird Base

1. Petal fold; repeat behind.

2.

3. Completed Bird Base.

Squash Fold

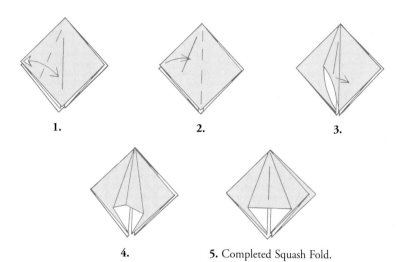

1. **2.** **3.**

4. **5.** Completed Squash Fold.

Rabbit Ear

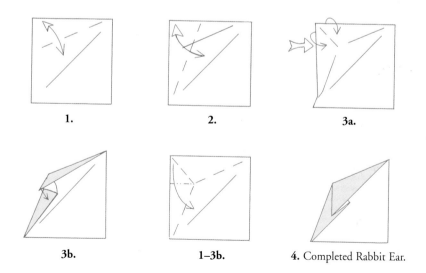

1. **2.** **3a.**

3b. **1–3b.** **4.** Completed Rabbit Ear.

Double Rabbit Ear

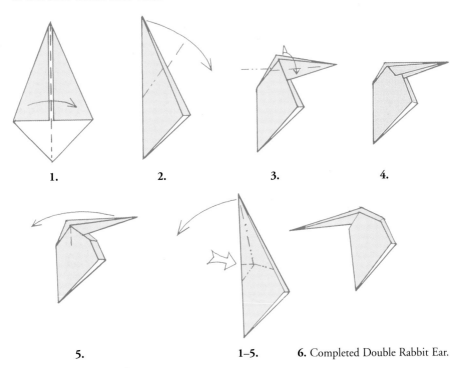

1.   **2.**   **3.**   **4.**

5.   **1–5.**   **6.** Completed Double Rabbit Ear.

Stretch Fold

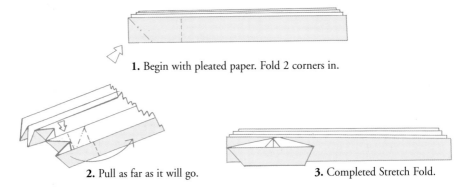

1. Begin with pleated paper. Fold 2 corners in.

2. Pull as far as it will go.

3. Completed Stretch Fold.

Fish Base

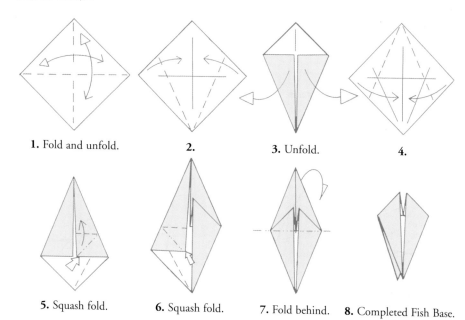

1. Fold and unfold. **2.** **3.** Unfold. **4.**

  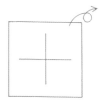 

5. Squash fold. **6.** Squash fold. **7.** Fold behind. **8.** Completed Fish Base.

Water Bomb Base

1. Fold and unfold. **2.** Fold and unfold. **3.** **4.** Fold and unfold.

5. **6.** Bring horizontal. **7.** **8.** Completed
Water Bomb Base.

Reverse and Crimp

Inside Reverse Fold

  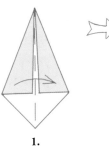  

1. **2.** **3.** Completed Inside Reverse Fold.

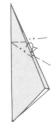 

2. **3.** Completed Outside Reverse Fold.

Outside Reverse Fold

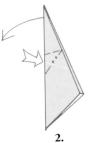 

2. **3.** Completed Inside Crimp Fold

2. **3.** Completed Inside Crimp Fold

Inside Crimp Fold

2. **3.** Completed Outside Crimp Fold.

Pentagon   Use a paper cutter for a clean cut

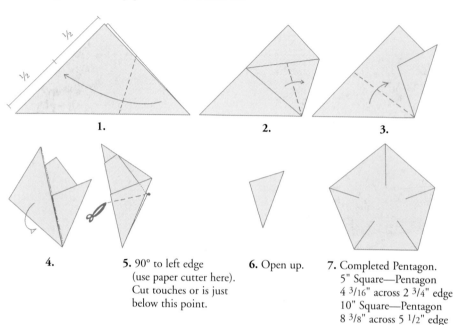

1.   **2.**   **3.**

4.

5. 90° to left edge (use paper cutter here). Cut touches or is just below this point.

6. Open up.

7. Completed Pentagon. 5" Square—Pentagon 4 3/16" across 2 3/4" edge 10" Square—Pentagon 8 3/8" across 5 1/2" edge

Hexagon   Use a paper cutter and a 30° to 60° triangle.

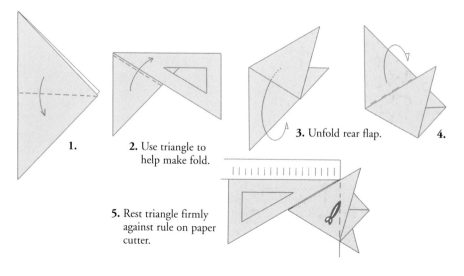

1.

2. Use triangle to help make fold.

3. Unfold rear flap.

4.

5. Rest triangle firmly against rule on paper cutter.

Part One

The Projects, Home Decor

Everyday objects have long been a source of inspiration for craftsmen and artists. Since ancient times, urns, and bowls have been embellished with decorative designs to make using them a pleasure. And such quotidian items as baskets and tableware have inspired artists to create still lifes that celebrate their simple charms. Nature is also a long-standing subject for artisans, who have represented it, particularly in the form of birds and flowers, in everything from household *objets* to sculpture.

It is from this wealth of subject matter that the models in this book were selected. The down-to-earth beauty of a well-made basket, the graceful stance of a crane, and the perfect symmetry of a star are all represented in this section. Their beauty is captured and preserved in origami models intended to adorn and enliven the home.

The projects in this section are arranged according to level of difficulty, but novice folders shouldn't be deterred from trying some of the more complex designs. The secret is to not let yourself get frustrated, but to continue to persevere until the art of folding comes naturally and instinctively. Rated on a scale of 1 to 4, the following would apply: Napkin Cuffs, 1; Classic Napkin Folds, 1; Pajarita, 1; Ingenious Letter-Fold, 1; Star, 1; Crane, 2; Fancy Dish, 2; Picture Frame, 2; Renaissance Shopping Bag, 2; Perching Birds, 2 and 3; Tropical Flowers, 2 and 3; Chalice, 3; Heart Gift Box, 3; Bowl, 3; Three-D Greeting Cards, 3; and Modular Folds, 4.

Napkin Cuffs

These are extremely simple and beautiful models and should provide a springboard to create your own variations. Created by Catherine Abbot, they enliven any table setting and particularly lend themselves to oriental and Latin meals. Some women may even be tempted to wear them as bracelets. In the line drawings, Cuff #1 refers to the narrow, brown and pink model; #2 refers to the wider, blue and pink cuff; and #3 is the crested, brown and orange model.

Napkin Cuff #1 (brown and pink)

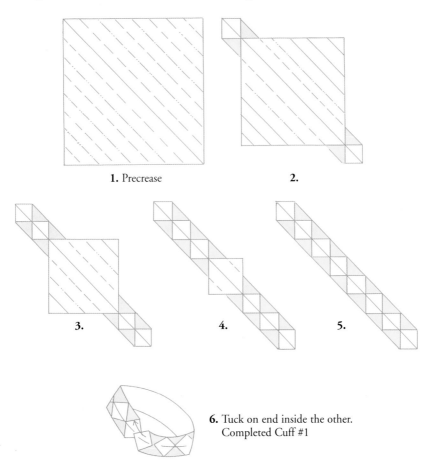

1. Precrease

2.

3.

4.

5.

6. Tuck on end inside the other.
   Completed Cuff #1

Napkin Cuff #2 (blue and pink)

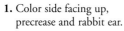

1. Color side facing up, precrease and rabbit ear.

2.

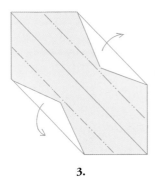

3.

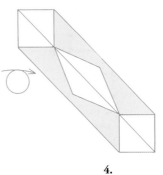

4.

5. Tuck one end inside the other. Completed Cuff #2.

Napkin Cuff #3 (brown and orange)

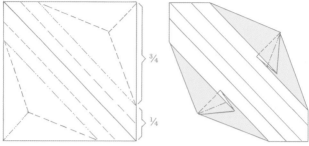

1. White side facing up, precrease then rabbit ear.

2. Squash rabbit ears

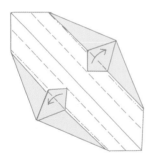

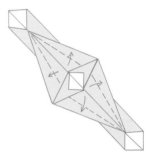

3. Valley fold, squash flaps, then accordion pleat model.

4. Valley fold top layers only. Tuck one end inside the other as in Napkin Cuff #2, step 5. Completed Cuff #3.

Classic Napkin Folds

Any restaurateur knows the value of the classic look of a table adorned with uniformly folded napkins. I have provided two designs for this purpose, created with ordinary table linen, not paper—unless of course, you want to add an amusingly formal note to a children's birthday party. The Bird of Paradise is a popular fold used in many restaurants. The Shawl comes from Gay Merrill Gross, an origami artist who has a special interest in the art of napkin folding. This design looks lovely when folded from a napkin with scalloped or decorative edges.

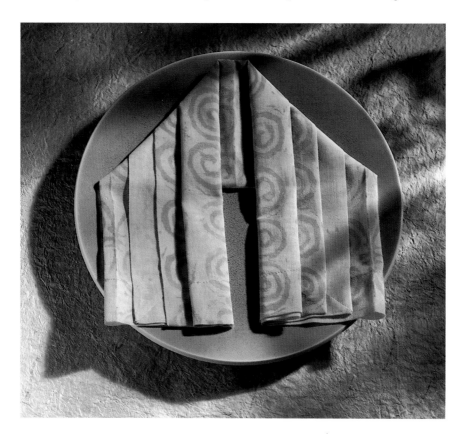

Shawl

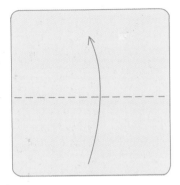

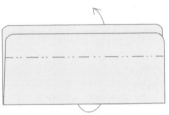

1. Begin with an open napkin. Bring the bottom edge up to around 1/2" below the top edge.

2. Fold the bottom edge behind so it extends around 1" beyond the top edge of the napkin.

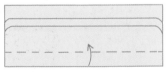

3. Fold up the bottom edge to create a hem around 1" wide.

4. The napkin now looks like this. Grasp the bottom edge and flip the napkin over so that hem that was at the bottom is now at the back of the top edge.

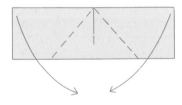

5. Place a finger at the center of the top edge and fold down each half of the top edge so that they meet at the horizontal center of the napkin.

6. Completed Shawl. If you wish, overlap the the center edges slightly.

Bird of Paradise

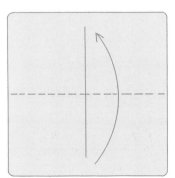

1.

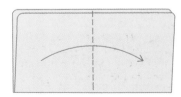

2.

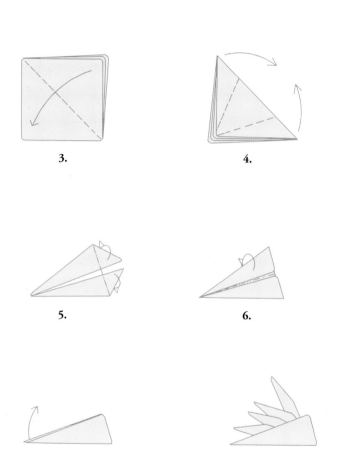

3.

4.

5.

6.

7.

8. Completed Bird of Paradise

Pajarita

The word pajarita is Spanish for "little bird." As its name implies, this design is of Spanish origin, although it is well known throughout Britain, France, and Germany. The base of this fold can be modified into several variations, such as a pinwheel or sampan. Like the Crane, the Pajarita looks beautiful in any variety of settings. I once saw a wedding cake decorated with wildflowers, pajaritas, and cranes.

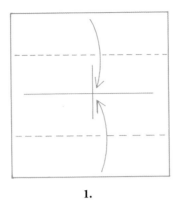

1.

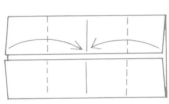

2.

3.

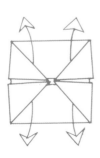

4. Pull out 4 corners.

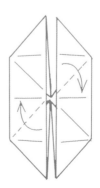

5.

6.

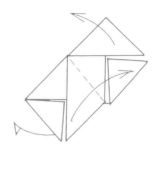

7.

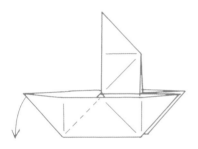

8. Outside reverse fold.

9. Completed Pajarita

Ingenious Letter-Fold

If you wish to send a special message through the mail, or want to show someone that you're thinking of them, consider making this simple combination envelope-stationery, in which the message is written directly inside the folds. A small piece of paper or flat object may also be enclosed. The envelope is perfectly suited to standard 8 1/2" by 11" paper. An instant classic, this design was created by origami master Robert Neale. And it can travel through the mail successfully, as I sent one myself to Neale.

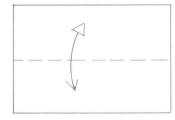

Start with rectangle.
1. Valley fold and unfold.

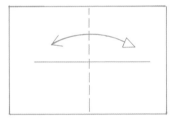

2. Valley fold and unfold.

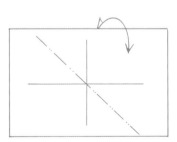

3. Mountain fold and unfold

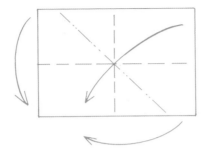

4. Collapse model.

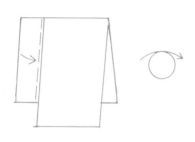

5. Valley fold and tuck into pocket. Turn over.

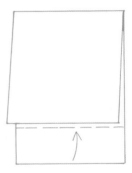

6. Valley fold and tuck into pocket.

7. Completed Letter Fold.

Star

Originally developed in Germany, the Star was imported to the United States by the Pennsylvania Dutch. It makes the quintessential tree decoration and a group of them might be fashioned into a mobile. The Star is made of four equal strips of paper, the dimensions of which should be 1" by 24".

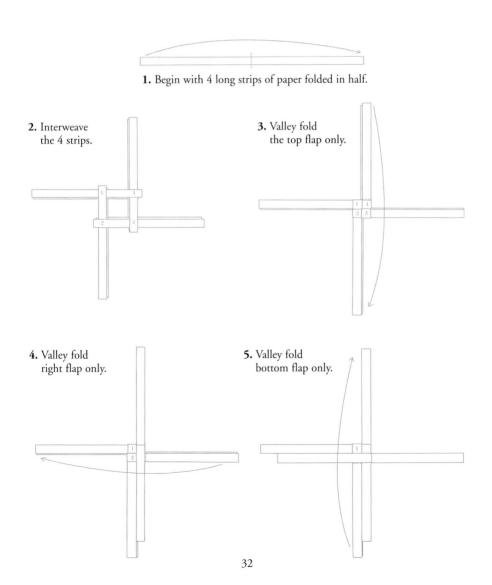

1. Begin with 4 long strips of paper folded in half.

2. Interweave the 4 strips.

3. Valley fold the top flap only.

4. Valley fold right flap only.

5. Valley fold bottom flap only.

6. Insert flap
into opening.

7.

8.

9.

10.

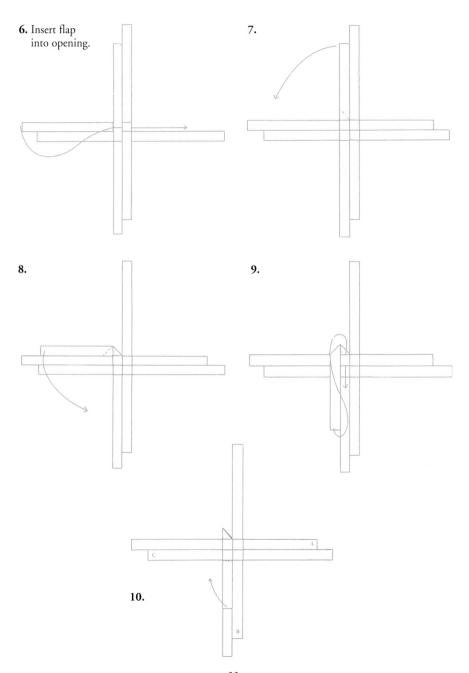

11.

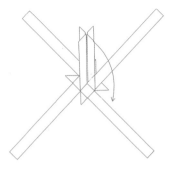

12.

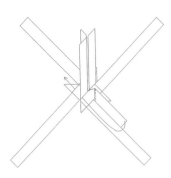

13. Cut off excess.

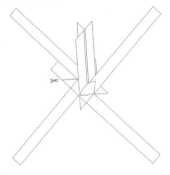

14.

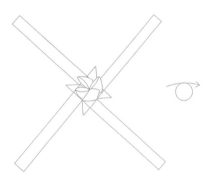

15. Repeat steps 7-13 with the other 3 flaps.

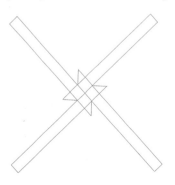

16. Completed Star.

Crane

This design is at least two hundred years old and is the most popular traditional Japanese model. It has become recognized as a symbol of peace ever since twelve-year-old Sadako Sasaki, a victim of radiation from Hiroshima, attempted to fold one thousand cranes as a gesture of universal peace. The Crane is attractive when displayed in a cabinet or on shelves, perhaps massed in groups for dramatic effect. It is also a nice addition to gift-wrapped packages. Use a 6-inch square of paper to create the design.

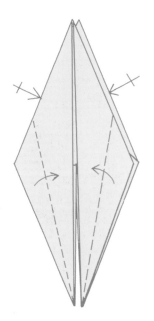

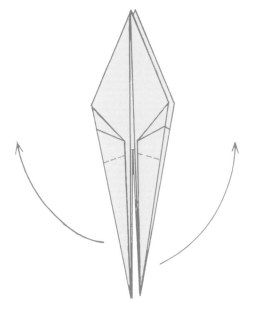

1. Begin with Bird Base.
Valley fold. Repeat behind.

2. Reverse fold.

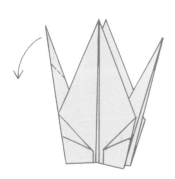

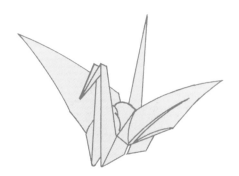

3. Reverse fold to form head.

4. Completed Crane.

Fancy Dish

Although it looks quite elegant, here is a very simple fold that has roots in both Japan and Argentina. In fact, it was one of the first models I learned how to do when I began folding as a child. Fill it with anything you wish, but be sure to display it prominently.

1. Fold 4 corners to center.

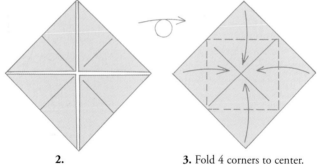

2.   **3.** Fold 4 corners to center.

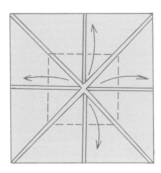

4. Fold out to edges.

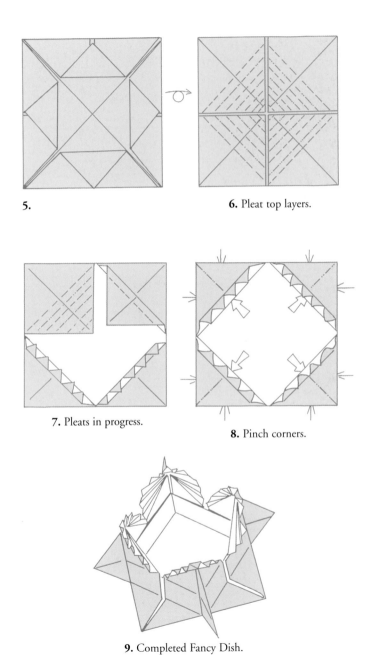

5.

6. Pleat top layers.

7. Pleats in progress.

8. Pinch corners.

9. Completed Fancy Dish.

Lotus Box

The lotus is a symbol of creation, and this lotus can be created anywhere there is paper. An ideal project to teach children who can then teach their friends! Use light-weight paper for best results.

Materials

Two sheets of 8" square paper, one green and one yellow
One 7 $^1/2$" square sheet of green paper

Lotus Box Tips

- Sharpen all creases with the side of your thumbnail to make them look neat and help them keep their shape longer.
- Create your squares from colorful magazine pages. The weight and size of magazine paper is ideal for this project.

The folding of the lid and the base are identical. The base paper is one-eighth smaller than the lid paper, so it will fit inside the finished lid. Begin with the largest green paper, with white side up.

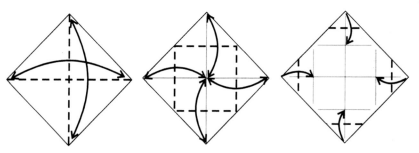

1. Valley fold paper in half, corner to corner, both ways. Unfold the paper to see that that two fold lines cross in the middle of the square.

2. Valley fold the four corners to the center of the square. Unfold the paper.

3. Valley fold the four corners of the square to the center of the fold lines created in the previous step.

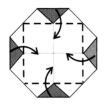  

4. Valley fold the green folded edges in, along the crease lines already made.

5. The models will now look like the illustration shown. Turn the models over.

6. (magnification) Valley fold the opposite side edges to the vertical center line of the square. Unfold.

7. Valley fold the top and bottom edges to the horizontal center line.

  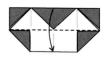 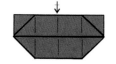

8. Flip up the lower flap to the top of the model to reveal the white side of the paper.

9. Valley fold the lower green corners to the square angled crease lines.

10. Return the flap to its original position. Repeat steps 7, 8, and 9 on the other side of the paper.

11. The model should now look like this. Open the model from the center.

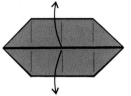 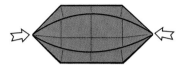

12. Push in the corners and square the four box walls.

13. Follow steps 1–12 to fold the smaller green paper for the lid. Both the lid and the base should match the drawing and one should fit inside the other.

14. Use the yellow square for the lotus top. Begin with the white side up. Fold the square in half, edge to edge, both ways.

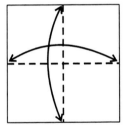 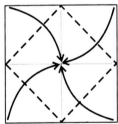 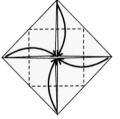

15.

16. Fold the four corners of the square to the center of the paper.

17. Fold the four new corners to the center. The model will look like the illustration and will have two layers of four yellow "petals" on this side.

18. (magnification) Fold the four petal corners of the first layer to the center of their outer edge.

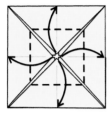 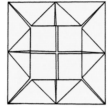 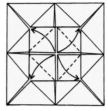 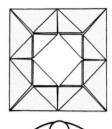

19. Model will look like the illustration.

20. Fold the petal corners of the second (inner) layer to the framed corners of the model.

21. Model will look like the illustration. Turn the model over.

22. Fold the corners of this square to the center.

   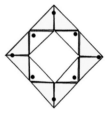

23. Unfold and set at right angles to the square base. These are the base points.

24. Turn the model over.

25. Slightly elevate the eight petal points marked by dots in the drawing. This is the lotus form.

26. Insert the four base corners into the open edges of the box lid.

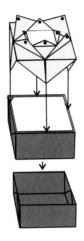

27. The finished lotus box.

Lotus Box Gallery

Here the lotus box is used as a photo frame. Unfold the lotus and insert a photo or a slip of contrasting colored paper, then refold with the element enclosed.

Fold several smaller lotus elements and insert them into the opening of the main lotus. You can experiment with colors and make more petals with a few scissor cuts.

Standard origami papers come in a wide variety of colors and patterns. All can be used—and in any combination—for the lotus box.

Picture Frame

A unique way to frame a print or favorite photo is with this simple frame. Created by Aldo Putignano, it is one of this repertoire of frame designs. The print or photograph simply slips into the pocket at the center of the heart. It also has the added feature of a stand-up base to hold the photo upright. You may need to cut the photo slightly to fit the frame.

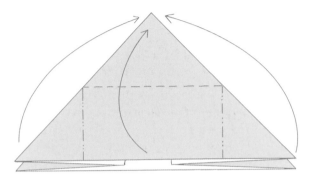

1. Begin with Water Bomb Base. Color side up.

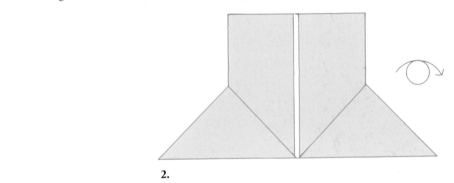

2.

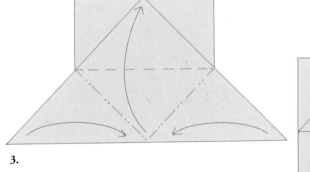

3.

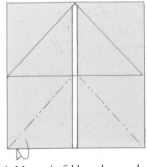

4. Mountain fold top layer only.

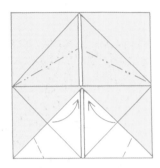

5. Lift top layer and squash.

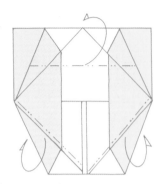

6. Mountain fold top to center.
Mountain fold bottom in between layers.

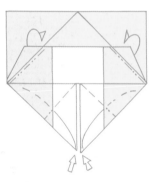

a. Mountain fold top in between layers.

b. Reverse fold.

c. Rotate 180°.

d.

7.

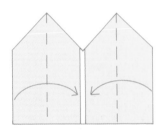

8. Valley fold single layer to center.

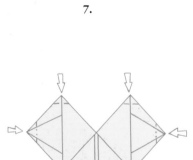

9. **a.** Reverse fold all corners.
b. Valley fold slightly.

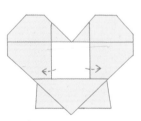

10. Insert photo. Completed Picture Frame.

Renaissance Shopping Bag

The shopping bag is a "renaissance" origami model in that it is both beautiful and functional. To further recommend it, the bag is easy to fold and can be made from virtually any large rectangle, at least 8 1/2 by 11 inches. Provided the paper is sturdy, it can actually carry quite a bit. To increase its usefulness, use a paper punch to add holes to the bag or add metal grommets; then attach a fancy cord for a handle. The artist who created the bag, Fred Rohm, attests to its popularity among avid shoppers. The bag can also be displayed in the home, perhaps filled with such decorative objects as dried flowers or marbles, or it can act as a container for gifts.

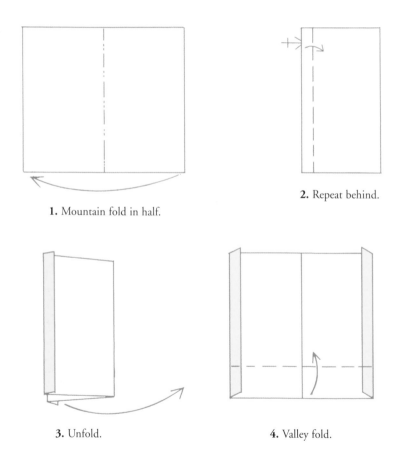

1. Mountain fold in half.

2. Repeat behind.

3. Unfold.

4. Valley fold.

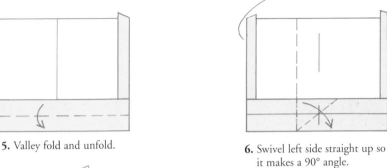

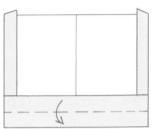

5. Valley fold and unfold.

6. Swivel left side straight up so it makes a 90° angle.

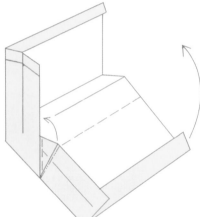

7.

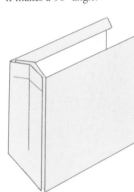

8. Repeat steps 4–7 on opposite side.

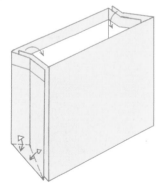

9. Fold outer lip over inner lip to lock in place. Crease sides.

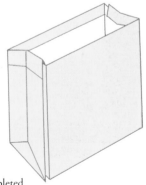

10. Completed Renaissance Shopping Bag.

Perching Birds

Referred to by one origami enthusiast as "notable for superb taste and artistry rather than for heavy-handed engineering," the work of the late Ligia Montoya is immensely appealing and elegant. Montoya, an Argentinian, pursued her own, original form of origami. It is a privilege to present this small representation of her work here. The photographs depict a parrot perched on a glass and a small swallow and a larger dove together on a roost. They can be displayed on a shelf or attached to a mobile. Birdcages have become a popular collectible for display in the home, and these origami models are also perfect ornaments for them.

Swallow

Start with Water Bomb Base.

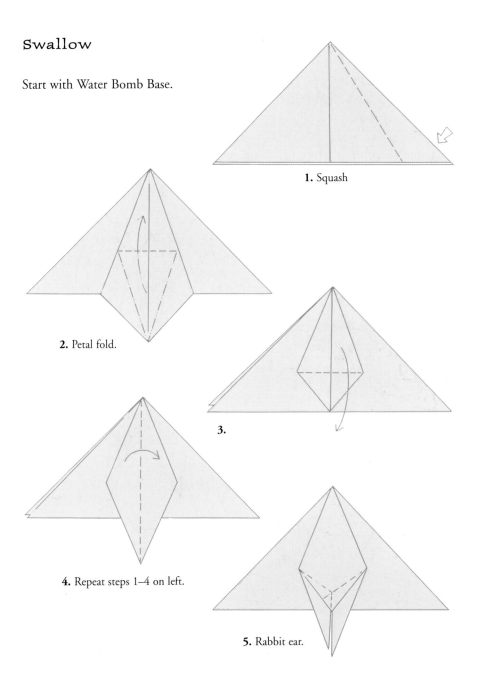

1. Squash

2. Petal fold.

3.

4. Repeat steps 1–4 on left.

5. Rabbit ear.

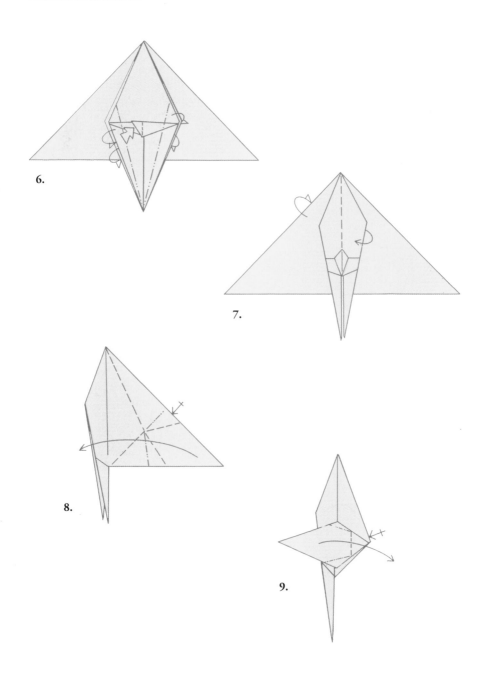

6.

7.

8.

9.

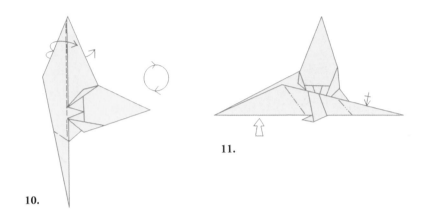

10.

11.

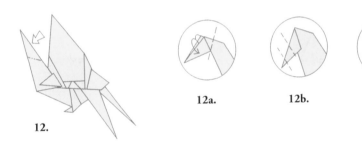

12.

12a.

12b.

12c.

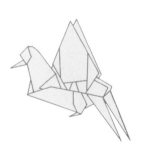

13. Completed Swallow

Flapping Dove

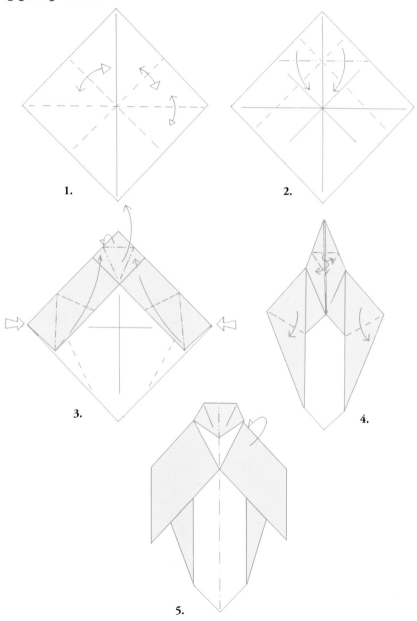

1.

2.

3.

4.

5.

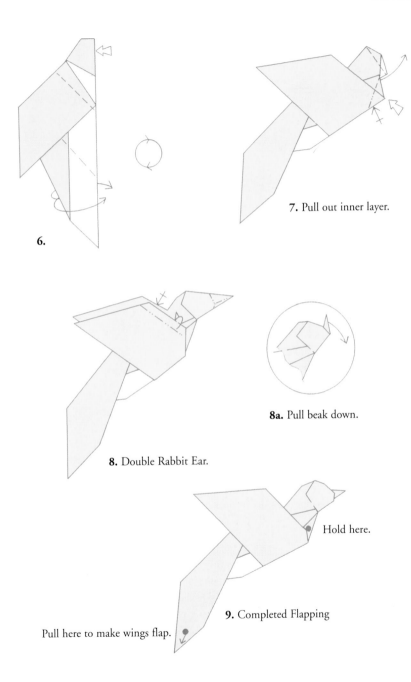

6.

7. Pull out inner layer.

8. Double Rabbit Ear.

8a. Pull beak down.

Hold here.

9. Completed Flapping

Pull here to make wings flap.

Tropical Flowers

One of the wonderful qualities of origami is its durability. When handled properly, designs can last forever. These fabulous flowers created by origami legend Ligia Montoya will never wilt and will bring beauty to rooms of your home year after year. Display them in a vase, add them to wreaths, or bundle them together with ribbon and simply display them on their sides. The photographs depict two types of flowers: a short-stemmed variety, grouped in a bowl, and a long-stemmed type, shown in a vase.

Long-stemmed Flower

Start with completed Pentagon.

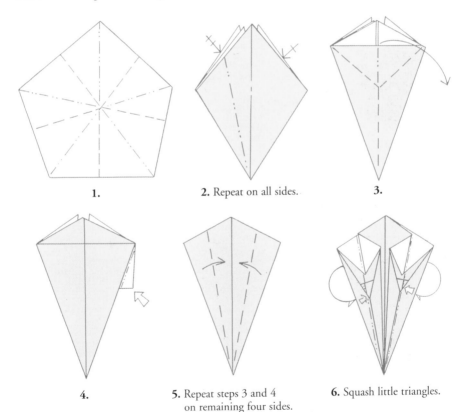

1.

2. Repeat on all sides.

3.

4.

5. Repeat steps 3 and 4 on remaining four sides.

6. Squash little triangles.

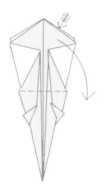

7. Fold out all five flaps slightly.

8. Finished flower.

Short-stemmed Flower

Start with step 6 of Pentagon

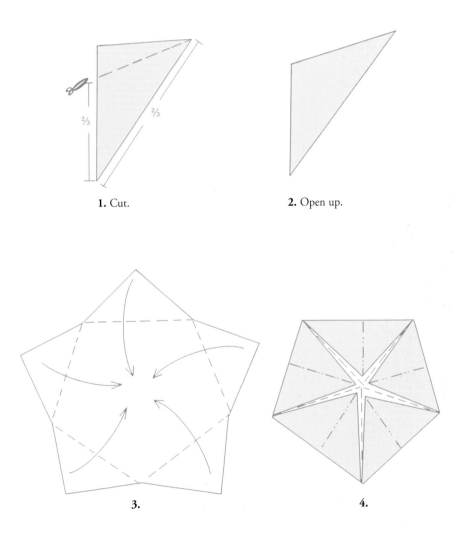

1. Cut.

2. Open up.

3.

4.

  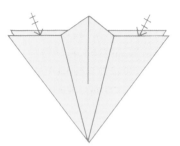 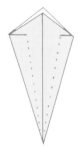

5. Squash fold.

6. Repeat on remaining four sides.

7. Squash inner flaps. Model will become 3-D.

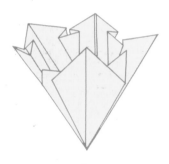 

8.

8a. Detail of inside. Petal fold all 5 points.

 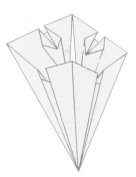

8b.

9. Finished Flower.

Chalice

This clever fold is from Samuel Randlett, a renowned champion of origami in the United States. The chalice is strikingly beautiful in itself, although it can also be filled with any number of objects—from nuts to paperclips. Randlett notes that a lid can be made to fit over the top of the cup by making a second chalice from a slightly larger piece of paper.

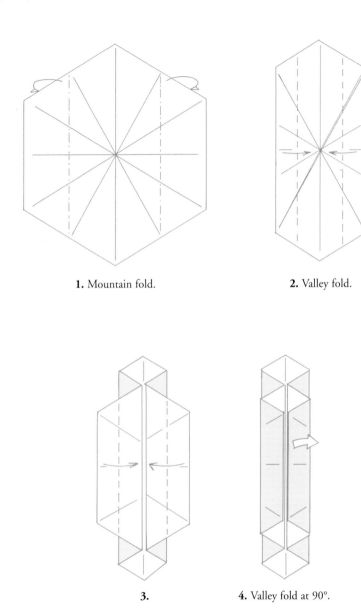

1. Mountain fold.

2. Valley fold.

3.

4. Valley fold at 90°.

Unfold and repeat steps 1–4 in the other two directions.

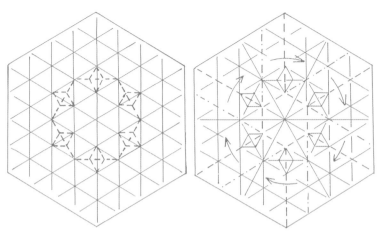

5. Form inner crease pattern.

6. Build on inner hexagon,
ignoring creases made in step 5.

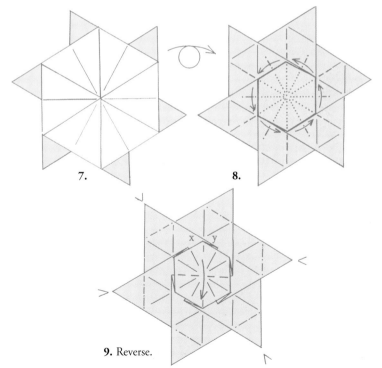

7.

8.

9. Reverse.

10. Squash fold on creases made in step 5.

11. Return x to y and repeat 5 times.

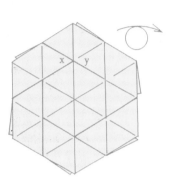

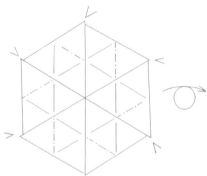

12.

13. Reverse fold.

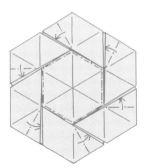

14. Tuck flaps into pockets.

15. Completed Chalice.

Heart Gift Box

Designed by Martha Mitchen, this charming fold is based on the Heart Valentine Card by Gay Merrill Gross. It begins with any 1" by 4 1/2" rectangle. The width of the box is equal to one half of the width of the paper, and the height is one-fourth the width. Keeping these dimensions in mind, the box can be made to a specific size. Any diminutive gift would be made more special when presented inside this delightful box. It would be the perfect container for an engagement ring.

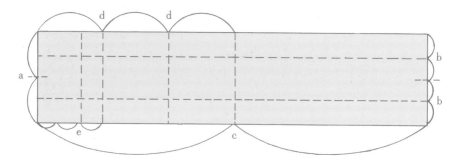

1. Fold a first, followed by b, c, d, and e.

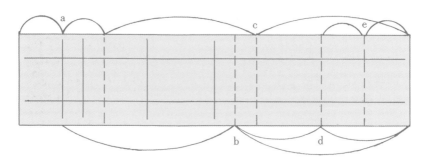

2.

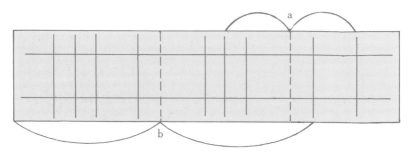

3.

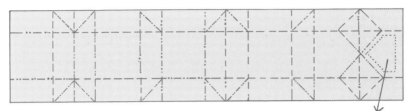

4. Insert paper slip with message: Be My Valentine xxx

*Be My
Valentine
xxx*

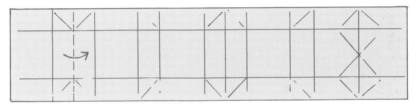

5.

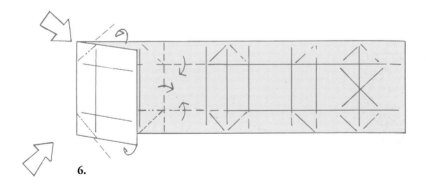

6.

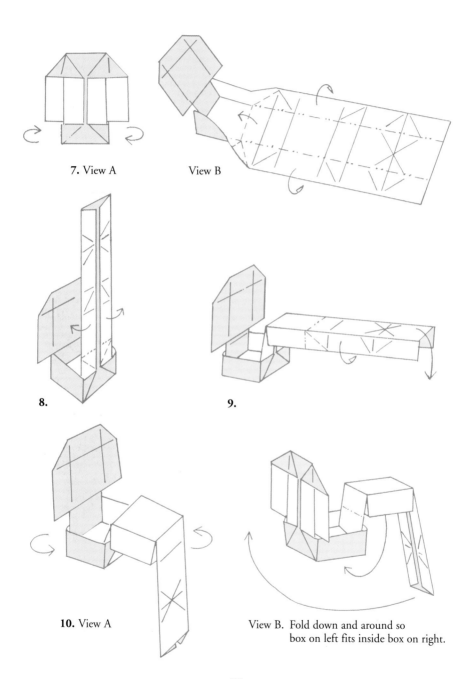

7. View A   View B

8.   **9.**

10. View A   View B. Fold down and around so
                                 box on left fits inside box on right.

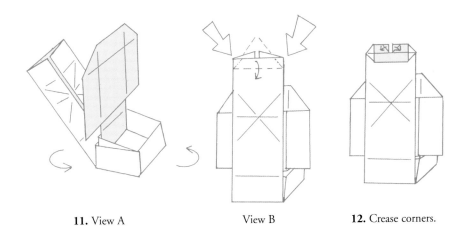

11. View A   View B   **12.** Crease corners.

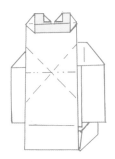

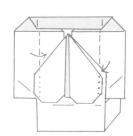

13. Fold as in Water Bomb Base.   **14.**   **15.** To lock front and back sections on top, tuck flaps into creases formed by water bomb base fold.

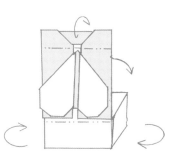

16. Fold down 90° to make flap on lid. Fold down 90° to form lid and close box.

17. Completed Heart Gift Box.

Bowl

This model makes a great centerpiece or simply a charming catch-all for anything from candies to hairbands. It is one of a number of bowls designed by Aldo Putignano. This charming model makes a lovely paper stand-in for the more expensive ceramic bowls. If you line the base with plastic or foil, it can serve as a unique container for diminutive potted plants. It is also a pretty potpourri container.

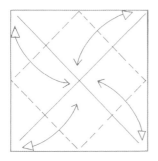

1. Fold and unfold

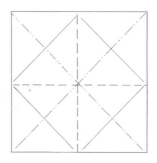

2. Make preliminary fold.

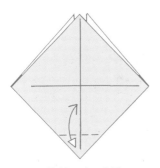

3. Fold and unfold.

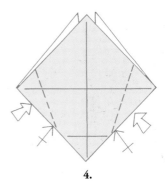

4.

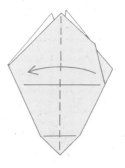

5. Reverse fold. Top flap only.

6. Top flap only.

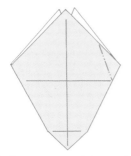

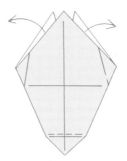

7. Repeat on remaining 3 sides

8. Open out.

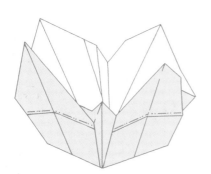

9. Fold all 4 sides inward.

9a. Detail of inside of flap.

10. Completed Bowl.

Three-D Greeting Cards

Aside from being attractive, these "pop-up" cards are meant to encourage letter-writing in lieu of omnipresent email. The cards incorporate the "dancing figure" from my personal letterhead. To make these designs, begin by photocopying the following pages and taping the copies over pieces of card stock. Then simply cut with an X-acto® knife along the indicated lines. Of course, using the same principles, you can fashion your own designs. They are a perfect personal touch for the holidays and other special occasions. They even have business applications—I once designed a card in this style for an architectural brochure.

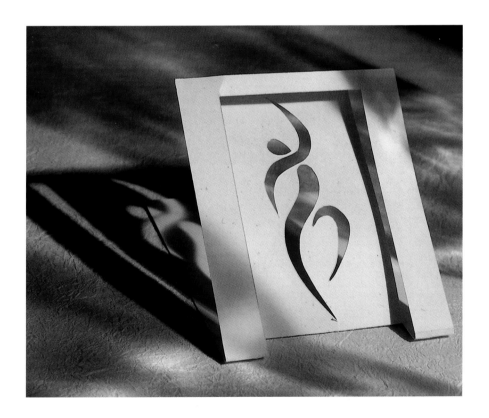

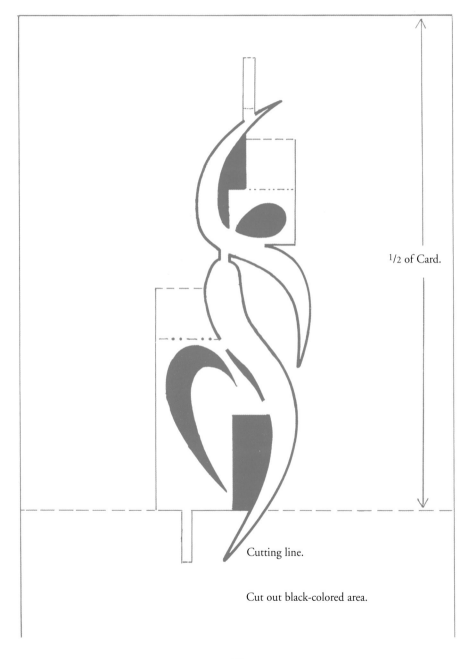

1/2 of Card.

Cutting line.

Cut out black-colored area.

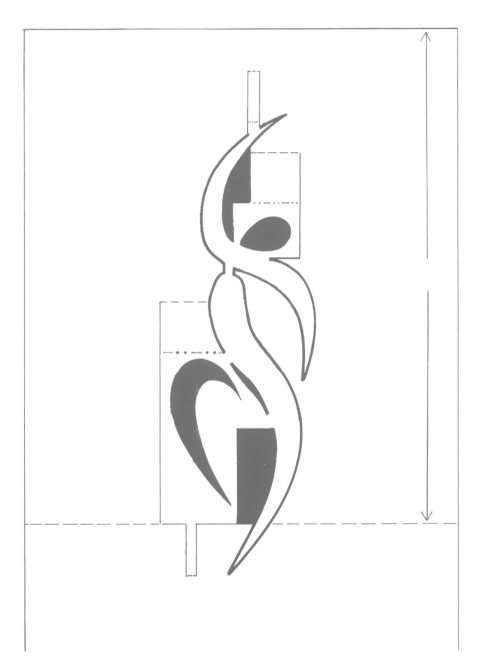

Modular Folds

These modular folds require a bit of patience to assemble, but they quickly become addictive. Strikingly sculptural, they can be displayed on tabletops or hung from the ceiling. They are especially magnificent lining the shelves of a sunlit room.

Origami artist Robert Neale calls this larger model a Star System. It is photographed here upon a table. The word "system" applies because there are so many variations and components—and so many design possibilities to explore. I have included only a few (Dr. Neale showed me several boxes filled with variations on this system). It may be helpful to use paper clips to hold the pieces together during construction.

The smaller model is called the Penultimate System and is photographed here grouped upon a desktop. It is a simple way of constructing polyhedrons. The structures are quite sturdy. It lends itself to variation and experimentation. The fact that the components fit together in a way to make the inside visible can be accentuated by placing the model near a light source or a solid background.

Penultimate System

Unit #1

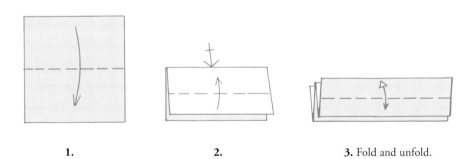

1.   **2.**   **3.** Fold and unfold.

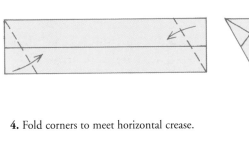 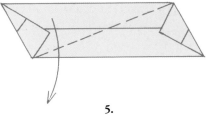

4. Fold corners to meet horizontal crease.   **5.**

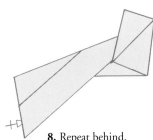 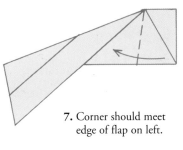

6. Unfold right flap.   **7.** Corner should meet
edge of flap on left.

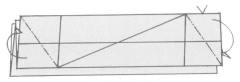 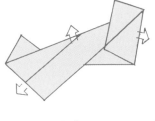

8. Repeat behind.   **9.** Open out to step 4.

10. Reverse folds.

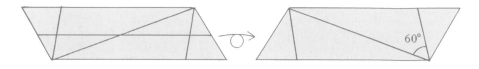

11.   **12.** Completed Unit #1.

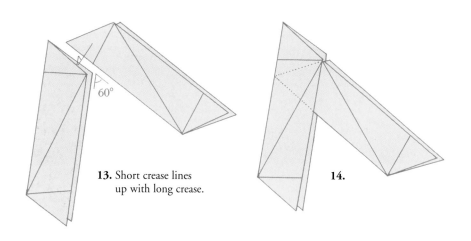

13. Short crease lines up with long crease.   **14.**

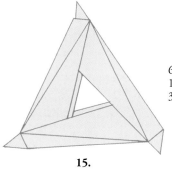

6 units form a tetrahedron.
12 units form an octahedron.
30 units form an icosohedron.

15.

Unit #2

Begin with step 4 of Unit #1

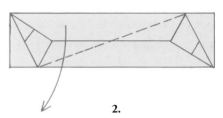

1. Corners should meet horizontal crease

2.

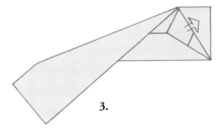

3.

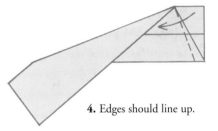

4. Edges should line up.

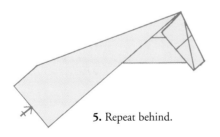

5. Repeat behind.

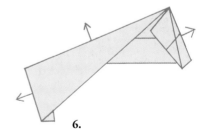

6.

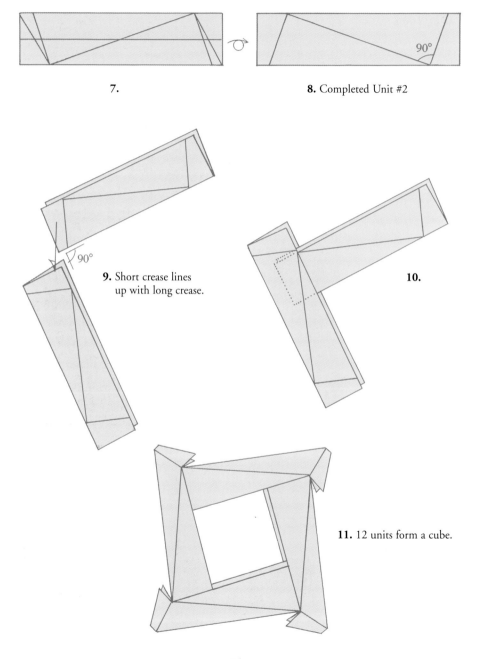

7.

8. Completed Unit #2

9. Short crease lines
up with long crease.

90°

10.

11. 12 units form a cube.

Unit #3

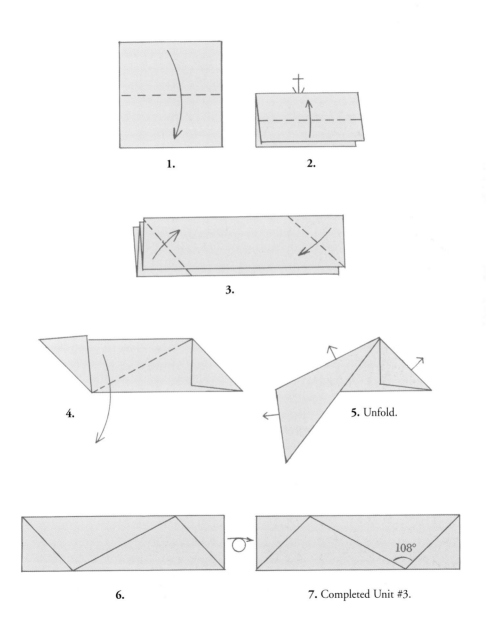

1.

2.

3.

4.

5. Unfold.

6.

7. Completed Unit #3.

108°

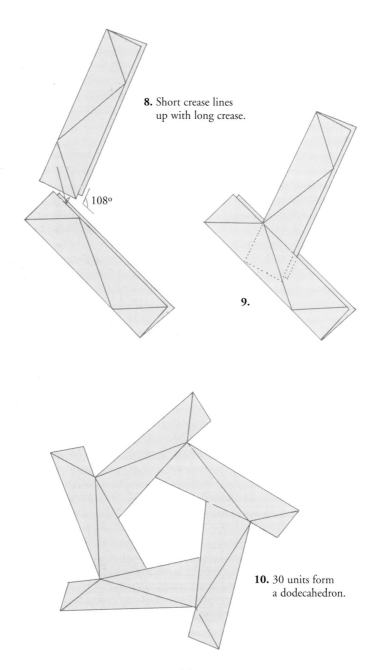

8. Short crease lines up with long crease.

108°

9.

10. 30 units form a dodecahedron.

Star System

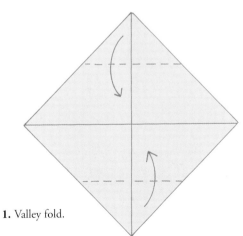

1. Valley fold.

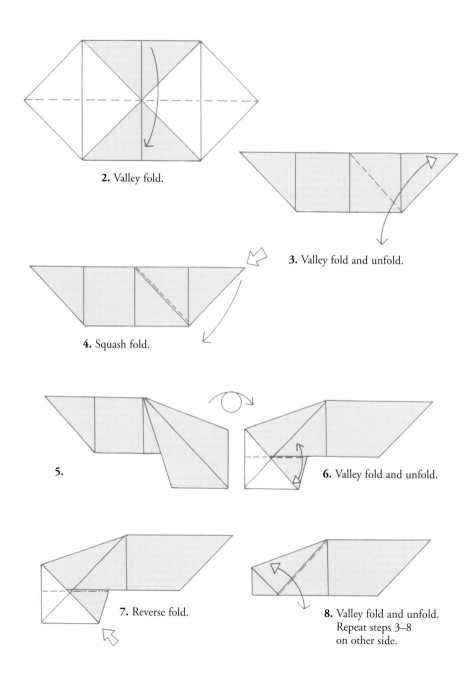

2. Valley fold.

3. Valley fold and unfold.

4. Squash fold.

5.

6. Valley fold and unfold.

7. Reverse fold.

8. Valley fold and unfold. Repeat steps 3–8 on other side.

9. Completed Star Module.

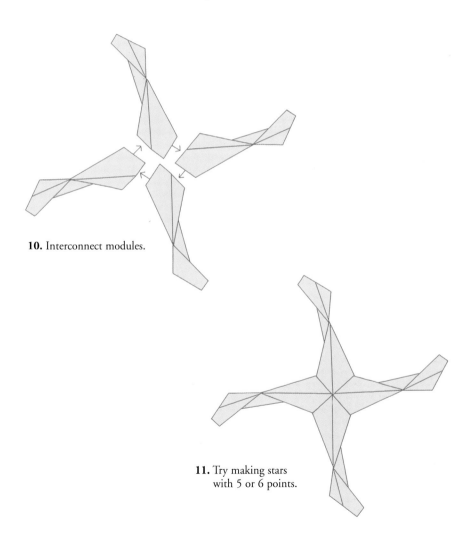

10. Interconnect modules.

11. Try making stars
with 5 or 6 points.

Variations

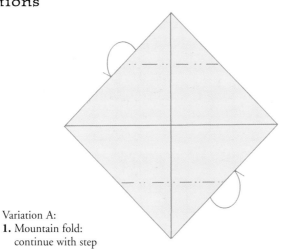

Variation A:
1. Mountain fold:
continue with step

Variation B:
2. Continue with step 2.

Part Two

The Projects, Mythical Creatures

Mythology, Art, and Origami

Human beings have always searched for meaning in the workings of the universe. The fantastic myths and folk tales of the Greeks, Celts, Native Americans, and other cultures are, on the simplest level, answers to what were at the time inexplicable phenomena. In a much deeper sense, the secrets of these legends and the beings that populate them continue to resonate within us, despite the influences of science and philosophy.

To my way of thinking, the need to express ourselves in artistic terms comes from the same part of our consciousness. For centuries, painters, poets, musicians, and other artists have challenged us to discover the story of ourselves, to find the common bonds that link us to each other and to our past. This is the role of the artist in society, and not one to be taken lightly.

As an art form, origami is unique in the limitations placed on the artist. It combines a sense of geometry and engineering with an artistic eye and more than a little dexterity. Origami is in one sense a game, a contest between the folder and the square. But hidden not too deep inside these creases is the simple secret that says a great deal about the structure of our universe and ourselves.

The models that follow represent some of the most magnificent mythical creatures imagined by a variety of cultures. Dragons are an especially popular motif, and they take on several intriguing forms in this section. Advanced students of origami should find them challenging to create, while novices may want to make the models in the order they are presented here—from easiest to most difficult. Rated on a scale of difficulty from 1 to 4, the following would apply: Ouroboros, 1; Wizard and Witch, 2; Winged Dragon, 3; Gargoyle, 3; Daedalus, 3; Pegasus, 3; Flapping Dragon, 3; Woodland Elf, 3; Centaur, 3; Rearing Dragon, 3; Shiva, 4; Unicorn, 4; Long-Tailed Dragon, 4; and Cerberus, 4.

Whatever your level of expertise, creating these mythical origami creatures should prove to be an absorbing and fulfilling experience.

Ouroboros

The worm eating its tail is a symbolic creature with ancient Egyptian and Greek origins. It was mainly used by the Gnostics to represent, broadly speaking, the eternal cycle of life. It also symbolizes completion and perfection. Ouroboros is sometimes depicted half dark and half light. In this sense, it is similar to the Chinese yin-yang symbol of counterbalancing opposing principles. I have developed a variation of Robert Neale's model to achieve the two-colored effect. The model looks best when the tip of the tail is touching the head and the crimp folds give the tail and neck a circular look.

3. Fold and unfold. Repeat behind.

1. Begin with fish base.　　**2.** Fold back and rotate.

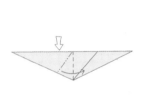

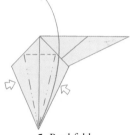

4. Squash fold.　　　　**5.** Petal fold.　　　　**6.** Repeat steps 4–5 behind.

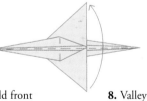

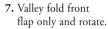

7. Valley fold front
flap only and rotate.　　　　**8.** Valley fold.

9. Alternate: Pull out one
layer to change color.　　　　**9a.** Valley fold.

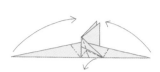

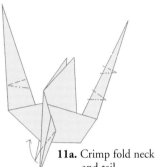

10a. Reverse fold both sides
　b. Rabbit ear. Repeat behind.

11a. Crimp fold neck
　　and tail.
　b. Reverse fold foot.
　　Repeat behind.

12. Reverse fold neck.
　　Reverse fold feet. Repeat behind.

13.

13a. Pull out loose paper
　　from inside. Repeat behind.

13b. Reverse fold.

14. Body should suggest circle.
　　Completed Ouroboros.

Bat

In China, the bat has long been a symbol of good luck. The image of the bat is a popular motif in oriental pottery, fabric and building decoration. A dwelling with bats is considered fortunate. It is also, of course, the perfect Halloween decoration or package ornament.

1. Cut or fold a square of paper diagonally in half—this will create a triangle of the proper proportions to begin this project. Any size will do.

2. Valley fold the triangle in half by bringing the two 45-degree angles together as shown. Unfold. This creates a centerline.

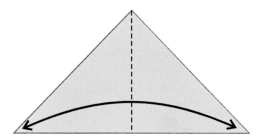

3. Valley fold all three corners to meet at the end of this center line where it touches the center of one of the triangle's sides. Unfold. You will now have a set of valley creases, as pictured.

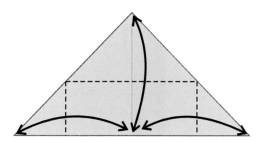

4. Valley fold the two 45-degree angle corners to the square corner.

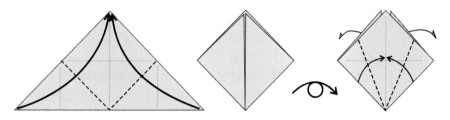

5. Turn the paper over. Notice how this square shape has two open edges and two folded edges.

6. Focus on the two folded edges of the square for the next step: Fold each of these edges to the center line and allow the triangular points from the underside to rotate around to the front of the paper.

7. The model should now resemble the photo. Pay particular attention to the mountain creases, which bisect each of the triangular shapes in front.

8. Grasp one of the mountain creases, align it with the center of the model, and Valley fold the paper between the mountain crease and the center line of the model. Do the same with the other mountain crease.

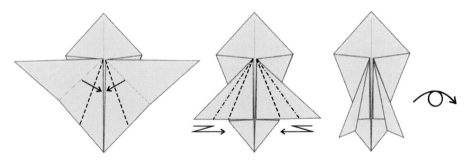

9. Mountain and valley fold the resulting paper triangles. Again, the model should resemble the photo.

10. Turn the model over.

11. Check to be sure that you have the correct side of the paper by looking at the center line: it should be a valley fold. Open up the model.

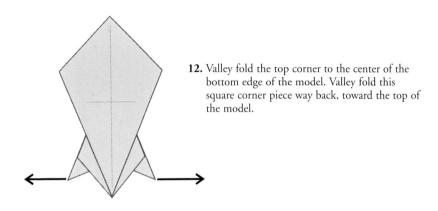

12. Valley fold the top corner to the center of the bottom edge of the model. Valley fold this square corner piece way back, toward the top of the model.

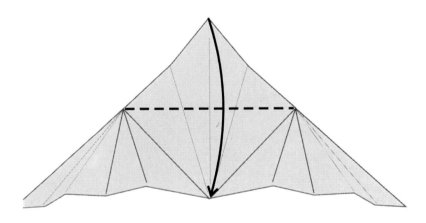

13. Notice the black dots at the end of the crease lines in the diagram. Align the end of each of the two crease lines with the folded edge of paper on their way up (dot-to-dot in the diagram). This will show you how far to fold the corner back up.

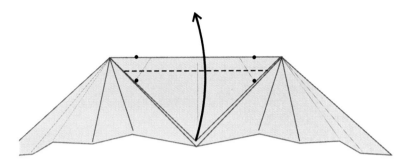

14. Create a scalloped edge along the bottom of the wings by setting in the indicated mountain and valley folds (optional).

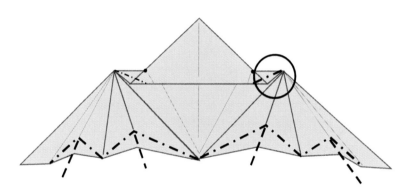

15. Mountain fold the left and right arm-edges (see the circle diagram for detail) under and out of sight.

 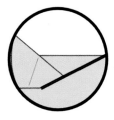

16. Mountain and valley fold the top corner to make the nose and head. Fold the nose first and then valley fold the whole shape down. Fold the wings closed over the body. Use the diagram in step 17 as a guide.

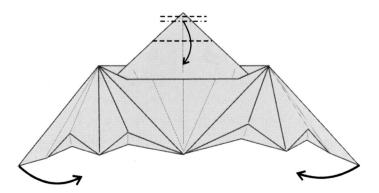

17. Mountain fold the arms in half lengthwise, beginning from the corner point and working inward until you hit a mountain crease in the area of the body. Swing this mountain crease up to touch the nearest ear corner and valley fold the paper between them.

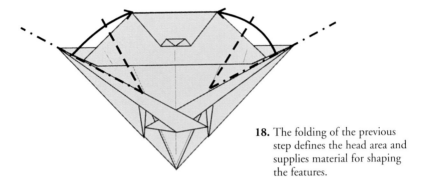

18. The folding of the previous step defines the head area and supplies material for shaping the features.

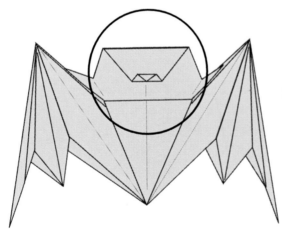

19. Mountain fold along the paper edge that runs from ear point to ear point.

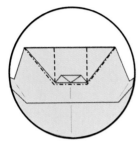

20. Valley fold the two ear points across the top of the head and make them stand straight up.

21. Twist the ear points so that the flat sides face forward (optional).

22. Open the mouth using a toothpick or similar tool (also optional).

23. Open the wings out and tightly curl the end of each wing around a toothpick to shape. You may wish to make a few roosting bats by folding the wings closed.

Wizard and Witch

Origami artist Robert Neale has the gift of being able to express a great deal in simple terms. Simplicity is, after all, at the heart of the concept of origami. In these models, such details as arms and legs are only suggested and the heads are exaggerated, but all this seems to accentuate their charm. These are neither the witches of Macbeth stirring the cauldron, nor Merlin of Arthurian legend; instead, these little gems resemble children in Halloween costumes.

Wizard

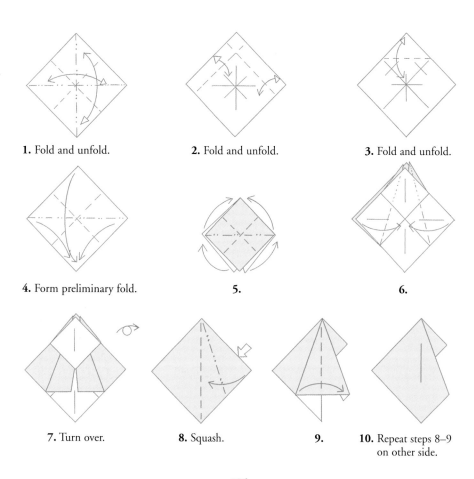

1. Fold and unfold.

2. Fold and unfold.

3. Fold and unfold.

4. Form preliminary fold.

5.

6.

7. Turn over.

8. Squash.

9.

10. Repeat steps 8–9 on other side.

11. Turn over.   **12.**   **13.** Crimp fold.   **14.**
                                        Crimp fold.
                                        Fold under flap.

14a. Squash fold head.   **15.**   **16.** Repeat steps 14–15
                                               on other side.

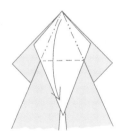  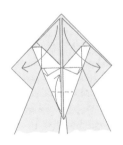

17. Petal fold.   **18.** Squash fold both sides.   **19.**

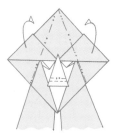

21a. Squash fold both
sides of nose.

20. Tuck inside pocket on
both sides. Crimp fold nose.

21. Crease nose to make 3-D.

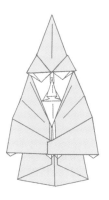

22. Make model 3-D
by creasing along lines.

23. Completed Wizard.

Witch

Follow steps 1–6 for Wizard.

7. Turn over.

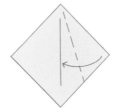

8.

9. Squash fold

10. Squash.

11.

12. Repeat steps 9–11 on other side

13. Turn over.

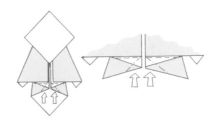

14. Squash fold both sides. Follow steps 14–19 of Wizard for head.

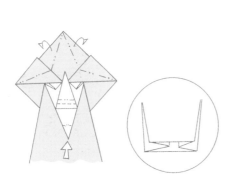

15. Tuck inside flap on both sides. Crimp fold nose. Close up of sink fold.

16. Crease nose to make 3-D as in Wizard step 21. Crease along fold lines. Tuck inside.

17. Completed Witch.

Winged Dragon

Another creation by Robert Neale, this Winged Dragon is a contemporary classic, with all the charm of a traditional model. I have found that altering the placement of the crimp folds in the neck and tail can actually change this dragon's character. This is probably my all-time favorite fold. It is a perfect example of what is enjoyable about origami.

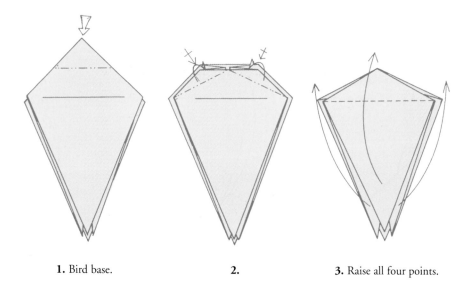

1. Bird base.　　　　　　**2.**　　　　　**3.** Raise all four points.

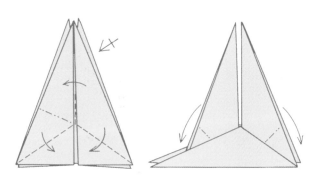

4. Rabbit ear. Repeat behind.　　　**5.** Reverse fold.

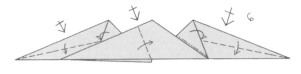

6.

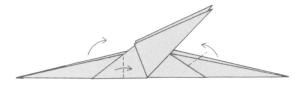

7.

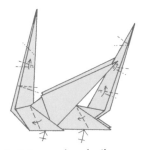

8. Crimp neck and tail.

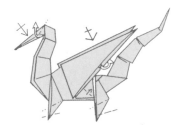

9. Lift one layer of the head. Repeat behind.

10.

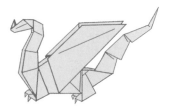

11. Completed Winged Dragon.

Gargoyle

Gargoyles are fantastic creatures of human or animal form. Originally, they were carved stone figures meant to frighten evil spirits away from churches. Today, they are often seen protruding not only from churches, but from older buildings of all kinds. Gargoyles are often as humorous as they are frightening. This creation by Jerry Harris is not unlike the monsters carved in stone. A funny-looking and slightly menacing beast, it is also a clever piece of origami, utilizing the rarely used blintzed frog base as a starting point.

Blintzed Frog Base

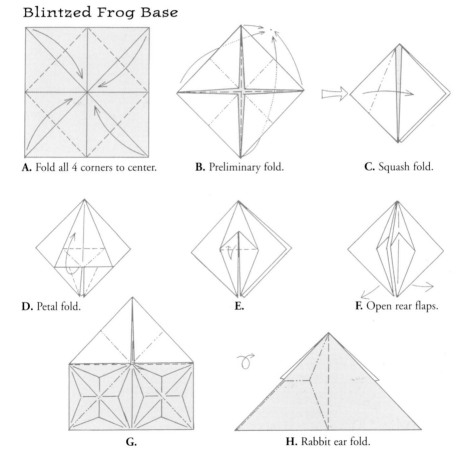

A. Fold all 4 corners to center.

B. Preliminary fold.

C. Squash fold.

D. Petal fold.

E.

F. Open rear flaps.

G.

H. Rabbit ear fold.

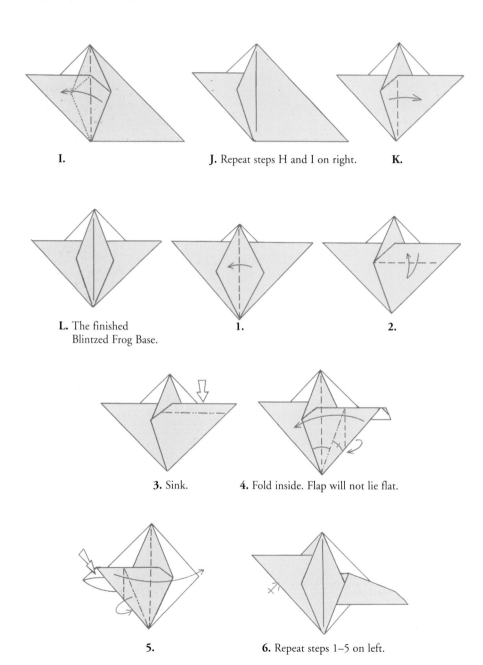

I.

J. Repeat steps H and I on right.

K.

L. The finished
Blintzed Frog Base.

1.

2.

3. Sink.

4. Fold inside. Flap will not lie flat.

5.

6. Repeat steps 1–5 on left.

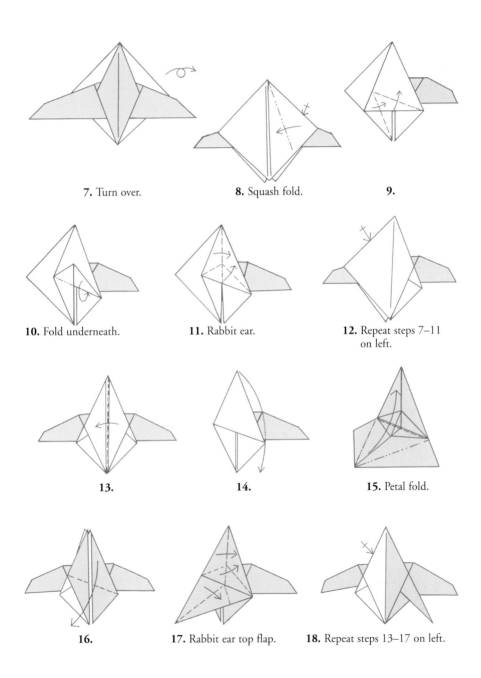

7. Turn over.

8. Squash fold.

9.

10. Fold underneath.

11. Rabbit ear.

12. Repeat steps 7–11 on left.

13.

14.

15. Petal fold.

16.

17. Rabbit ear top flap.

18. Repeat steps 13–17 on left.

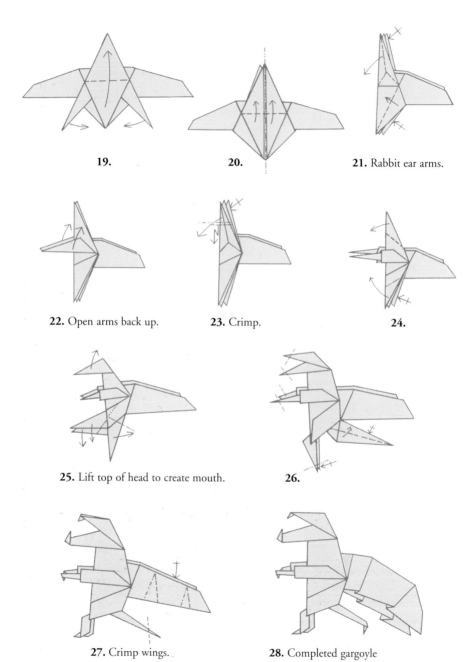

19.

20.

21. Rabbit ear arms.

22. Open arms back up.

23. Crimp.

24.

25. Lift top of head to create mouth.

26.

27. Crimp wings.

28. Completed gargoyle

Daedalus

Daedalus was a highly skilled builder, renowned for building the labyrinth for King Minos on the island of Crete. After losing favor with the king, Daedalus was imprisoned in a tower and decided that the best way to escape was to fly. He made a pair of wings for himself and a pair for his son, Icarus. During the flight, Icarus flew too close to the sun, which melted the wax that held the wings together, and fell into the sea and drowned. Daedalus flew to safety in Sicily. Gabriel Alvarez's Daedalus model is one of the most graceful and natural in all origami.

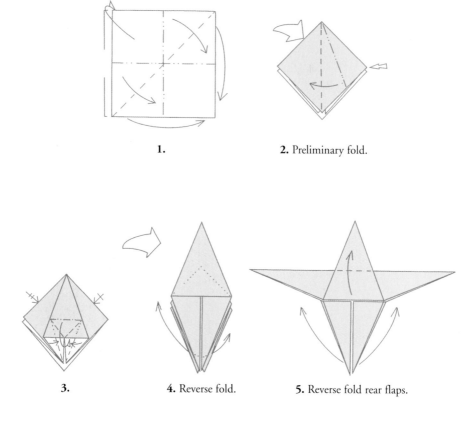

1.   **2.** Preliminary fold.

3.   **4.** Reverse fold.   **5.** Reverse fold rear flaps.

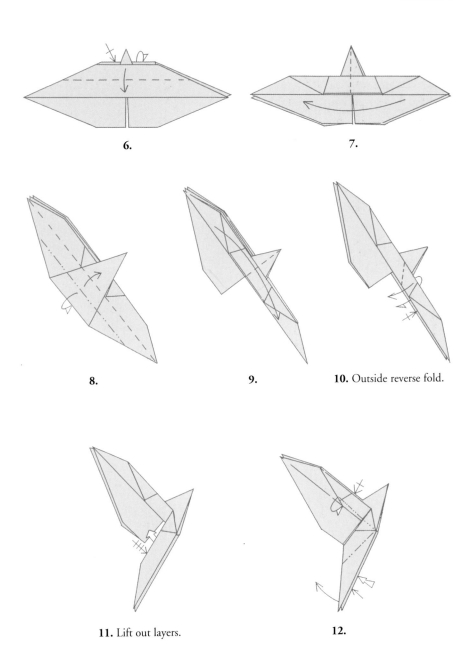

6.

7.

8.

9.

10. Outside reverse fold.

11. Lift out layers.

12.

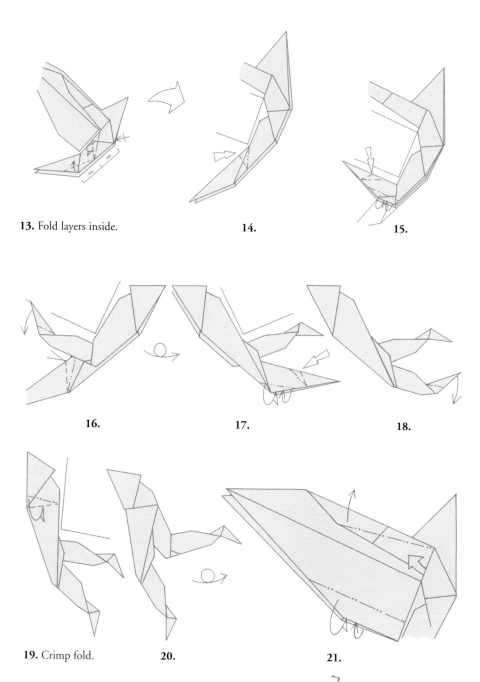

13. Fold layers inside.

14.

15.

16.

17.

18.

19. Crimp fold.

20.

21.

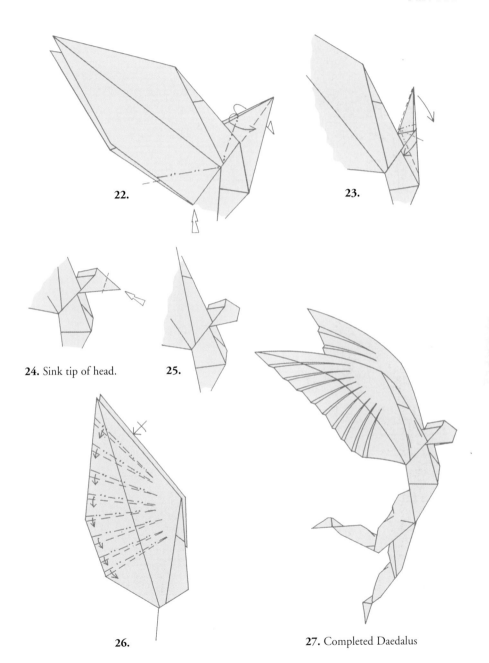

22.

23.

24. Sink tip of head.

25.

26.

27. Completed Daedalus

Pegasus

The winged horse is one of the most well-known figures of Greek mythology. Pegasus sprang fully formed from the body of Medusa the Gorgon, who was slain by Perseus. The fountain of Hippocrene on the Muses' mountain of Helicon was opened with a kick from his hoof. Many folders have tried their hands at Pegasus. The one presented here was created by Gabriel Alvarez and begins, like many of the others, with a blintzed bird base. The base provides the correct number of points to form the head, tail, legs, and wings. Alvarez has captured the beauty and stature of this gentle creature.

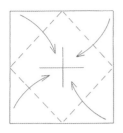

1. Fold 4 corners to center.

2. Preliminary fold.

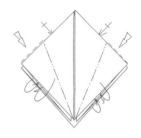

3.

4. Pull out loose flaps.

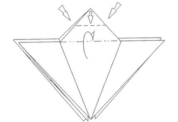

5. Partial sink.

6. Lift middle flaps.

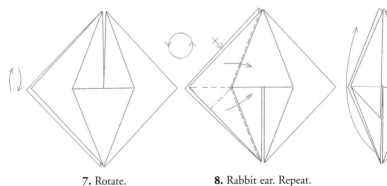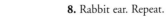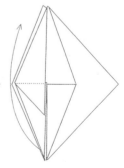

7. Rotate.

8. Rabbit ear. Repeat.

9.

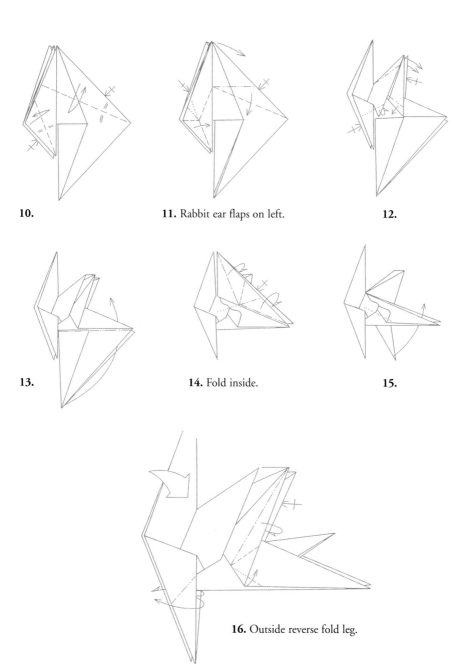

10.

11. Rabbit ear flaps on left.

12.

13.

14. Fold inside.

15.

16. Outside reverse fold leg.

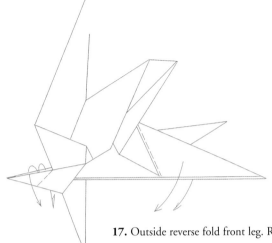

17. Outside reverse fold front leg. Reverse fold hind leg.

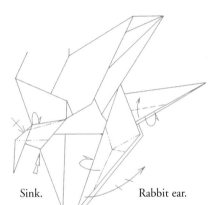

18. Sink. Rabbit ear.

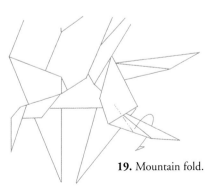

19. Mountain fold.

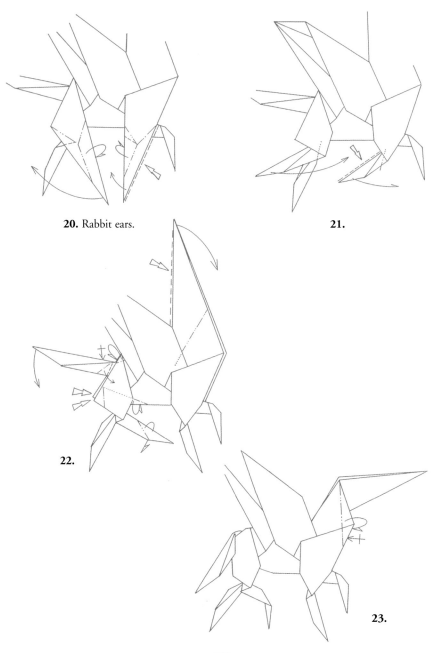

20. Rabbit ears.

21.

22.

23.

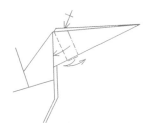

24. Crimp fold.   **25.** Outside reverse fold.   **26.** Pull out layers.

27.   **28.** Shape head.

29. Completed Pegasus.

Flapping Dragon

One of Stephen Weiss's specialties is coming up with figures that reflect the whimsical side of origami. Some of the most humorous pieces are the ones that can be made to actually do something. When this dragon is grasped at the bottom of the tail and lower neck and gently pushed a bit toward the middle, its wings will flap!

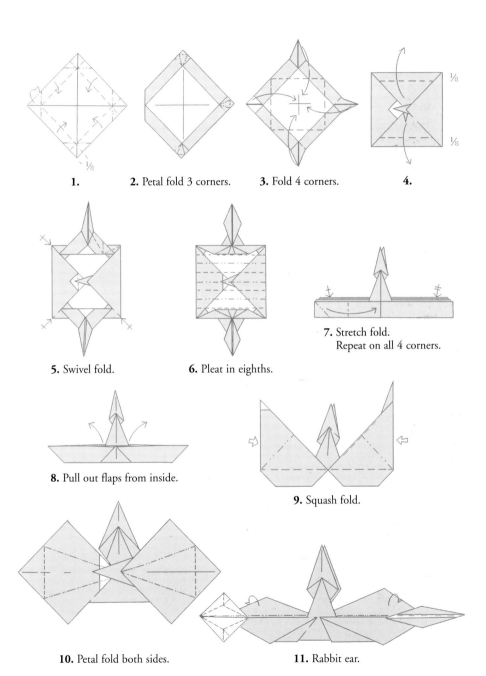

1.

2. Petal fold 3 corners.

3. Fold 4 corners.

4.

5. Swivel fold.

6. Pleat in eighths.

7. Stretch fold.
Repeat on all 4 corners.

8. Pull out flaps from inside.

9. Squash fold.

10. Petal fold both sides.

11. Rabbit ear.

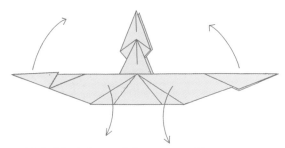

12. Pull both flaps on left. Mountain fold outer points up; this will bring inner points down.

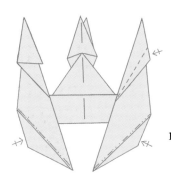

13a. Detail of inside of wing. Crimp fold. Repeat on opposite wing.

13b. Tuck under flap on other side. Repeat on opposite wing.

13. Mountain fold. Repeat behind.

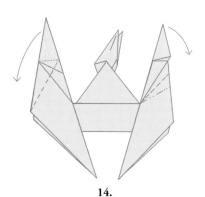

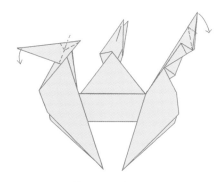

14.

15. Rabbit ear. Pull bottom jaw.

15a. Outside reverse fold.

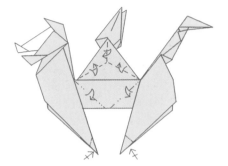

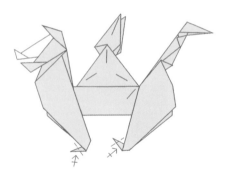

15b.

16. Reverse fold foot. Repeat on all 4 legs. Crease as shown.

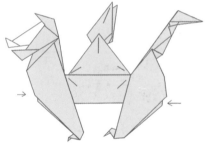

17. Reverse fold foot. Repeat on all 4 legs.

18. Completed Flapping Dragon. Push in at arrows to make wings flap.

Woodland Elf

This clever model, created by Stephen Weiss, is a good example of using pleated paper—a technique pioneered by Neal Elias. The use of pleated paper has opened up new possibilities in designing origami figures, although the proportions of certain models may require the use of rectangular paper. Here the arms and legs of the elf are stretched from the pleated base. Even today, people still believe in the "little people." When an old woman from Galway was asked if she believed in elves or leprechauns, she replied firmly, "No, but they're out there!"

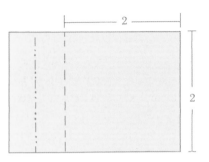

1. Use a 2" x 3" rectangle (or a rectangle with 2:3 proportions), color side up.

2. Pleat in sixteenths. Crease.

3. Pull single layer up 90º to long portion. Each pleat must be swiveled up and back on corresponding long pleat below it. Work back and forth from bottom to top, moving layer up a little at a time.

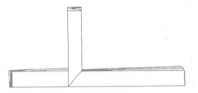

4. Starting from the third corner bottom on each side of leg pleats, stretch the pleats to separate the legs. Note that stretching brings all folded edges up even on top and the layer of the center will rise up from the bottom to allow this at the middle folded edge.

4a. Excess paper around the crotch is pushed in to wrap around vertical center edge of body as best it can.

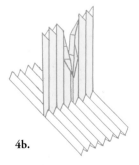

4b.

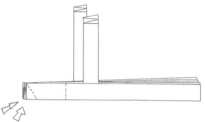

5. Stretch one arm.

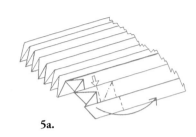

5a.

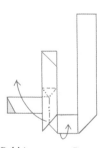

5b. Repeat behind.

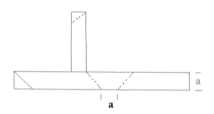

a

6. Make 2 ordered 90° reverse folds with layers even on both sides. Note that the distance **(a)** between reverses equals the width of one pleat.

7. Rabbit ear arm. Repeat behind. Color change base by wrapping a single layer to the outside on each side. Then open base out flat.

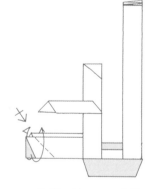

8. Outside reverse fold.

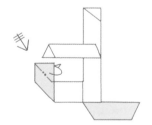

9. Mountain fold all 4.

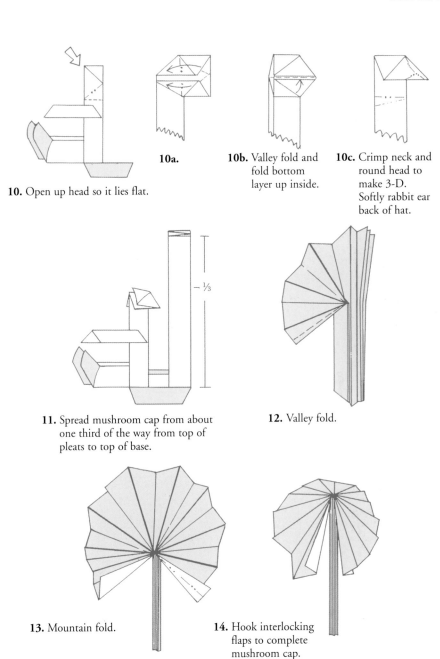

10a.

10. Open up head so it lies flat.

10b. Valley fold and fold bottom layer up inside.

10c. Crimp neck and round head to make 3-D. Softly rabbit ear back of hat.

− ⅓

11. Spread mushroom cap from about one third of the way from top of pleats to top of base.

12. Valley fold.

13. Mountain fold.

14. Hook interlocking flaps to complete mushroom cap.

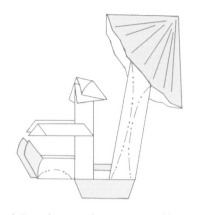

15. Mountain fold joint to lock. Mountain fold edges to round out mushroom, fold corners underneath.

16. Round out mushroom stem and legs.

17. Completed Woodland Elf.

Centaur

A centaur has the upper body of a human and the lower body of a horse. Cheiron, the most famous centaur, was the instructor of Achilles and other distinguished legendary Greek heroes. Cheiron is seen in the night sky as Sagittarius, the Archer. Neal Elias's interpretation of the centaur is quite ingenious. It is made from a rectangle whose length is twice its width, of any size.

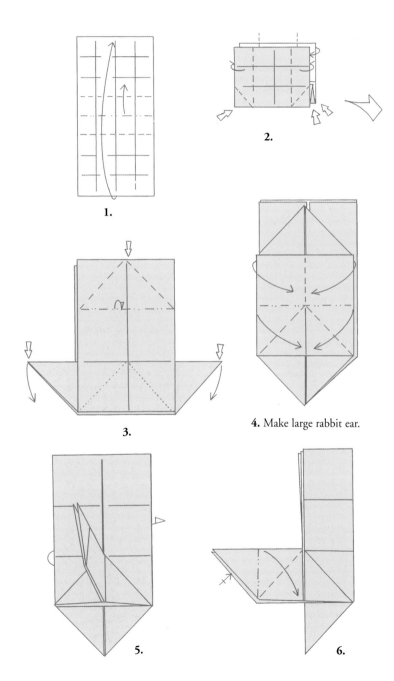

1.

2.

3.

4. Make large rabbit ear.

5.

6.

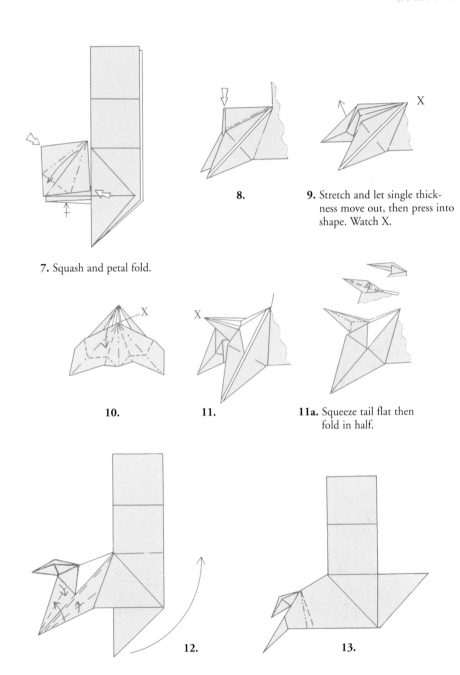

8.

9. Stretch and let single thickness move out, then press into shape. Watch X.

7. Squash and petal fold.

10.

11.

11a. Squeeze tail flat then fold in half.

12.

13.

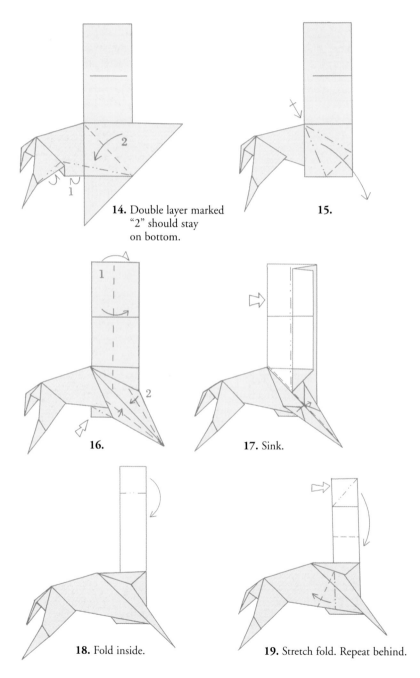

14. Double layer marked "2" should stay on bottom.

15.

16.

17. Sink.

18. Fold inside.

19. Stretch fold. Repeat behind.

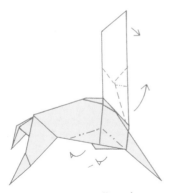

20. Rabbit ear. Pull out loose paper.

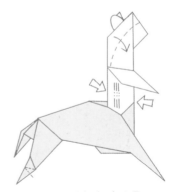

21. Make body 3-D.

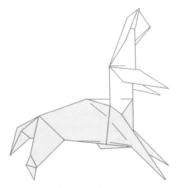

22. Completed Centaur.

Rearing Dragon

This model by Marc Kirschenbaum is a variation on Robert Neale's Winged Dragon. The Rearing Dragon has more detail, however, especially in the head. The mouth opens menacingly, and its remarkably sinister-looking eyes are formed from the reverse side of the paper, all of which carry his distinctive stamp.

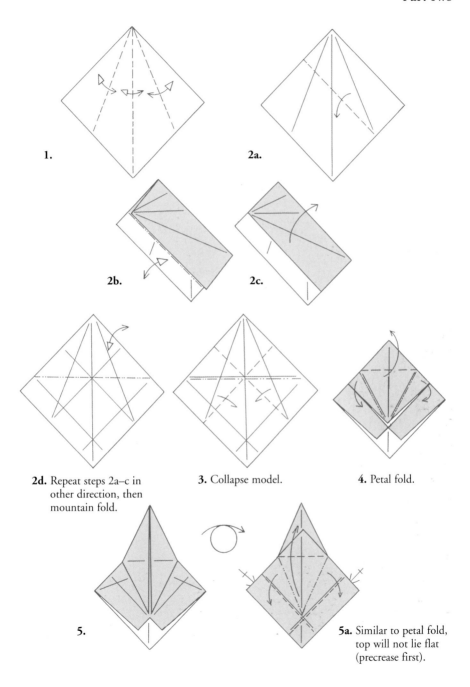

1.

2a.

2b.

2c.

2d. Repeat steps 2a–c in other direction, then mountain fold.

3. Collapse model.

4. Petal fold.

5.

5a. Similar to petal fold, top will not lie flat (precrease first).

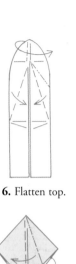 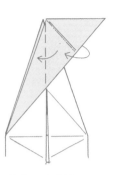  

6. Flatten top.

7. Squash fold.

 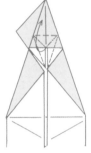

8. Squash fold.

9. Petal fold.

10. Fold over while reverse folding small flap at 45°. Repeat steps 8–10 on other side.

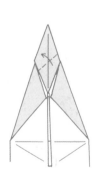 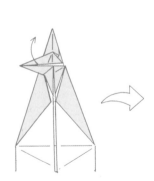 

11. Valley fold lightly.

12. Raise a layer.

13. Mountain fold corner. This will result in a color change at top of small flap.

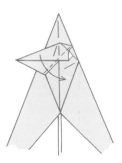

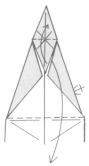

14. Return flap to position in step 11. Repeat steps 11–13 on other side.

15. Valley fold small flap up and valley fold large flap down. Repeat behind.

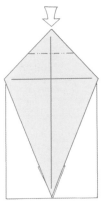

16. Sink top.

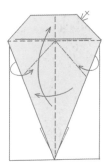

17. Fold in half while simultaneously bringing flap up. Repeat on other side.

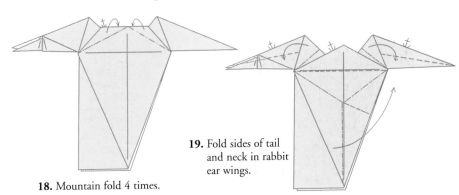

18. Mountain fold 4 times.

19. Fold sides of tail and neck in rabbit ear wings.

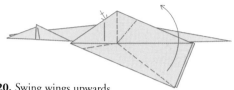

20. Swing wings upwards

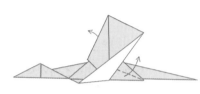

21. Valley fold up a layer of the triangle while pulling out a layer from the wings. Note: the wing must lie perpendicular to the bottom.

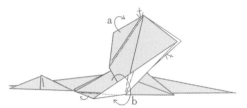

22. Note that (a) and (b) must be folded simultaneously.

22a. Back of wing.

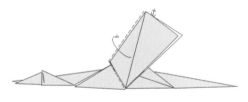

23. Wrap layers around wings.

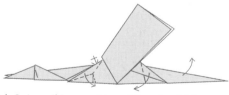

24. Swing tail into position while valley folding hind legs, rabbit ear front legs.

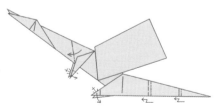

25. Reverse fold neck and flatten head. Crimp tail and round out feet and tail.

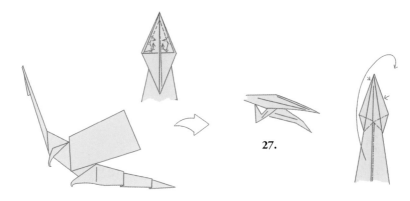

26. Bottom of head: form jaws so as to reveal the eyes and fold in sides of jaws.

27.

27a. Top of head: shape head and neck.

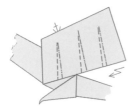

28. Crimp while curling wings.

29. Shape wings by using reverse fold.

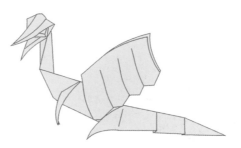

30. Completed Rearing Dragon.

Shiva

Shiva, the Hindu god known as "the Destroyer," is shown here in the guise of Nataraja, Lord of the Dance. This beautiful work by Robert Lang is quite a challenge to fold, particularly in the shaping of the arms and legs. But this is what gives the figure its distinctively Indian character. Lang has proven here that practically anything can be folded from a square of paper.

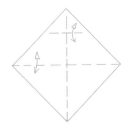

1. White side up; fold and unfold. Pinch.

1a. Pinch only.

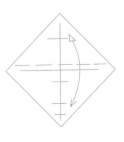

2. Fold and unfold all the way across.

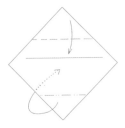

3. Fold points to last crease.

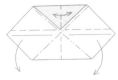

4. Make a hybrid preliminary fold/water bomb base.

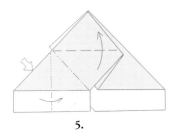

5.

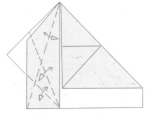

6. Crease angle bisectors.

151

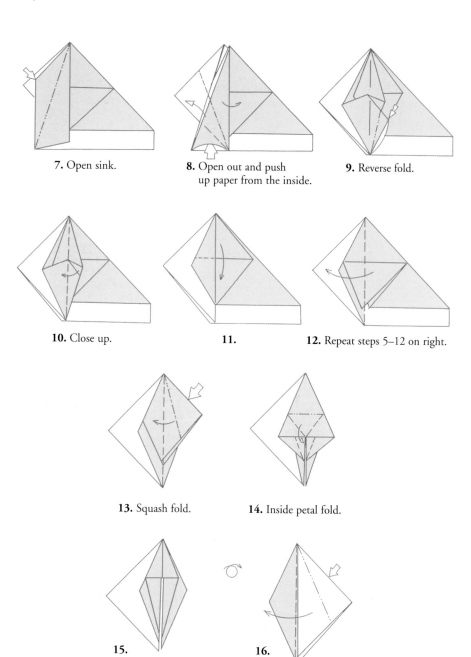

7. Open sink.

8. Open out and push up paper from the inside.

9. Reverse fold.

10. Close up.

11.

12. Repeat steps 5–12 on right.

13. Squash fold.

14. Inside petal fold.

15.

16.

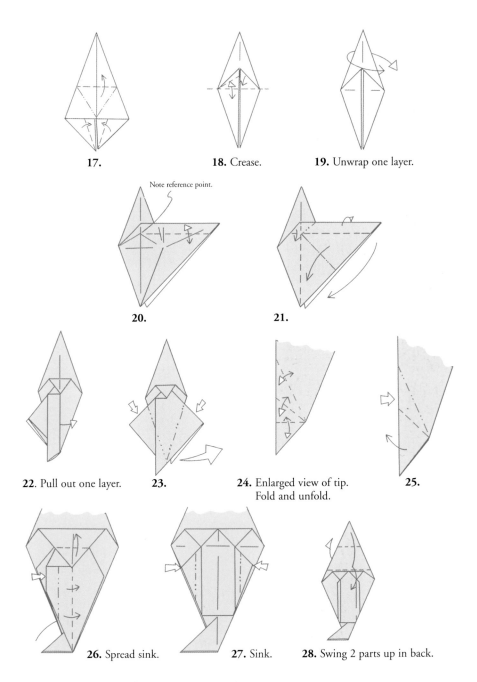

17.

18. Crease.

19. Unwrap one layer.

Note reference point.

20.

21.

22. Pull out one layer.

23.

24. Enlarged view of tip. Fold and unfold.

25.

26. Spread sink.

27. Sink.

28. Swing 2 parts up in back.

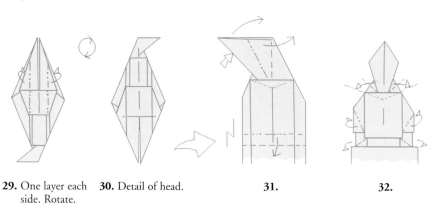

29. One layer each side. Rotate.

30. Detail of head.

31.

32.

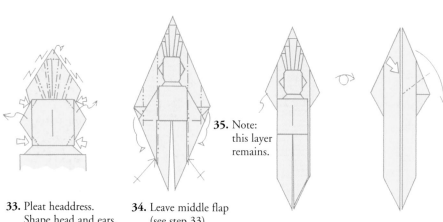

33. Pleat headdress. Shape head and ears.

34. Leave middle flap (see step 33).

35. Note: this layer remains.

36.

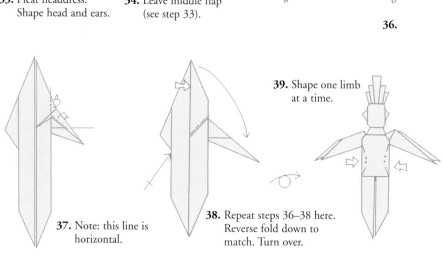

37. Note: this line is horizontal.

38. Repeat steps 36–38 here. Reverse fold down to match. Turn over.

39. Shape one limb at a time.

40. Front arm, right side of model (Shiva's left).

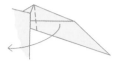

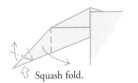

Squash fold.

41. Outside reverse fold.

42. Narrow and round arm. Sink tip of hand.

43. Left front arm

44. Round arm. Sink tip.

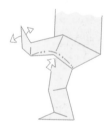

46. Round leg. Open at foot.

45. Left leg.

47. Right leg.

48. Round leg. Open at foot.

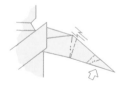

49. Right rear arm.

50. Shape.

51. Repeat steps 49–50 on left, except curl hand.

52. Completed Shiva.

Unicorn

The unicorn is well known as the gentlest, loveliest beast in legend. Artsits' depictions have varied from goat-like to horse-like in nature. Stephen Weiss has created a model whose equine features give grace and power to this horned wonder.

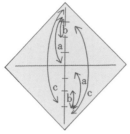

1.

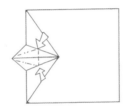

2. By folding the top and bottom corners to the creases made in step 1, the paper forms a 7" x 9" rectangle.

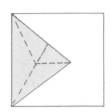

3. Rabbit ear.

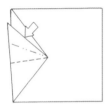

4. Squash fold tip.

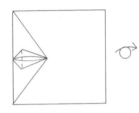

5. Petal fold.

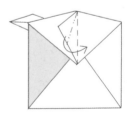

6. Valley fold.

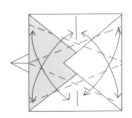

7. Fold corner to meet crease.

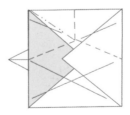

8.

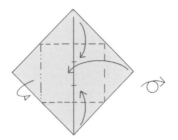

9. Squash fold.

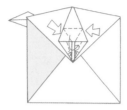

10. Inside petal fold flap.

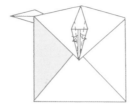

11. Crease.

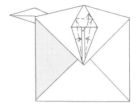

12. Using crease as a guide, petal fold, raising horizontal folded edge while folding sides in.

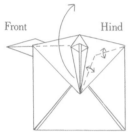

13. Valley fold front leg up crease, angle bisector on hind leg.

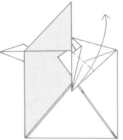

14.

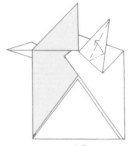

15.

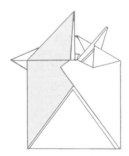

16. Swivel.

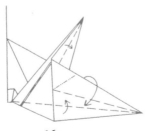

16a.

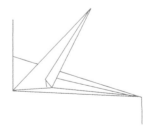

17. Repeat steps 8–16 on bottom.

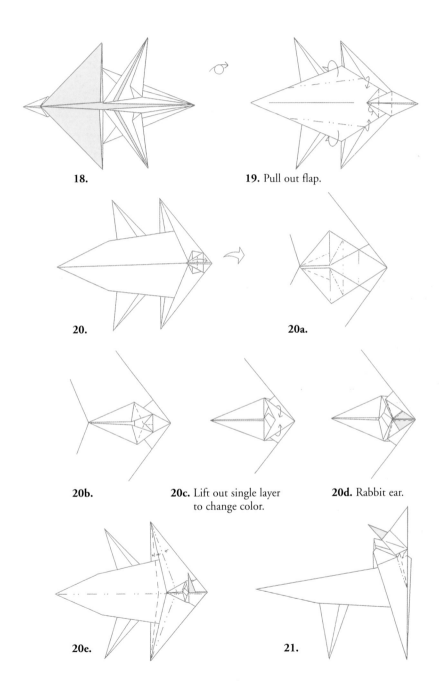

18.

19. Pull out flap.

20.

20a.

20b.

20c. Lift out single layer to change color.

20d. Rabbit ear.

20e.

21.

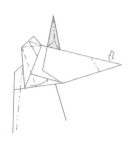

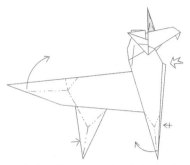

21a. Crease mane. Tuck under flap. Double rabbit ear to round out horn.

22. Rabbit ear repeat behind. Sink breast. Double rabbit ear. Repeat behind so leg points to the right.

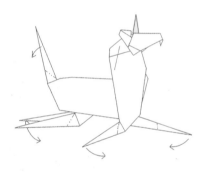

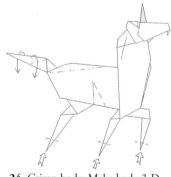

23. Mountain fold, repeat behind.

24. Crimp body. Make body 3-D.

24a. Squash. Repeat on lall 4 legs.

24b. Completed hoof.

25. Completed Unicorn.

Long-tailed Dragon

Matthew Green's dragon requires a good deal of patience, but the result will prove worthwhile. This dragon is of the winged lizard variety, with its thin body and long tail. This model requires foil paper in order to retain the folds and shape the figure.

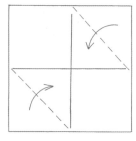

1. Color side up, precreased for Water Bomb Base.

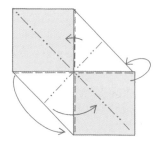

2. Refold along precrease as shown.

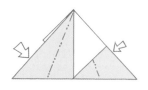

3. Squash fold front and back large points.

4. Fold up the bottom triangle; repeat behind.

5. Fold the corner of the left half of the top flap to the right, so that its bottom edge lines up with the white flap 2 layers beneath.

6. Fold the point back to the right, creasing along the vertical center crease of the model.

7. Fold the point's left edge to the center crease.

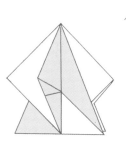

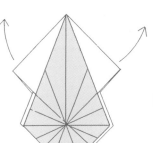

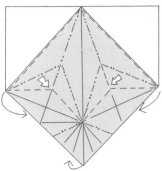

8. Repeat steps 5–7 on right, then on the back 2 flaps. Unfold.

9. Pull out the white corners to reveal all of the new creases.

10. Assemble as shown, both front and back.

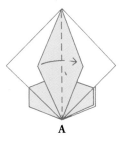

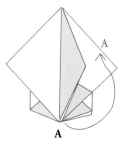

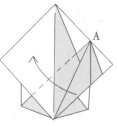

11. Fold the colored portion of the front in half.

12. Reverse fold up the point A.

13. Open up the top flap to reveal the corner of the paper.

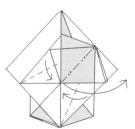

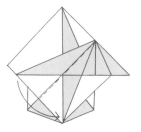

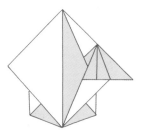

14. Form a rabbit ear fold by pinching and lifting the colored corner and folding in the edges along the precreases.

15. Fold the flap closed again.

16. Repeat steps 11–15 on the back.

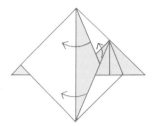

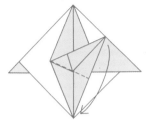

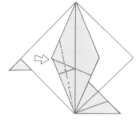

17. Pull one layer only from the right to the left, spreading open some inside creases.

18. Fold the whole flap down to the bottom.

19. Sink fold to narrow the left side.

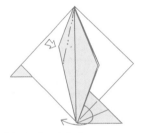

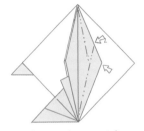

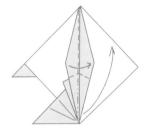

20. Again, sink then reverse fold the 2 inner layers and the pointed flap all the way to the left.

21. Repeat the two sinks on the right.

22. Fold the left half to the right, rotating up the triangular flap at the same time.

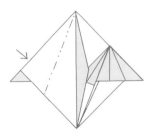

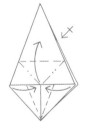

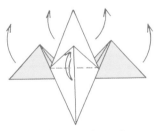

23. Repeat steps 17–22 on the back. Then, squash fold the white flaps.

24. Petal fold, front and back (only white portions shown here).

25. Fold the triangle on the center down and up again. Then, open up the white by pulling out the colored points on the sides.

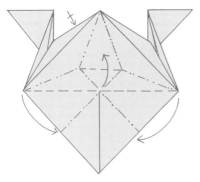

26. Form the front and back opened sections into half bird bases.

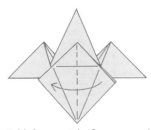

27. Fold the top right flap over to the left.

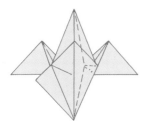

28. Rabbit ear fold the right flap, then undo and fold the flap to the left.

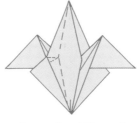

29. Repeat the rabbit ear along the same creases, reversing them, then undo.

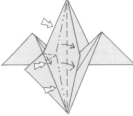

30. Perform a double rabbit ear, one on each layer of the top flap. At the same time, spread the flap open. You may need to reach inside.

31. Fold 2 layers from the left to the right.

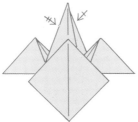

32. Repeat steps 27–31 on the left, then on remaining sides.

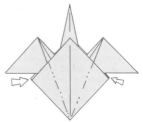

33. Reverse the sides in.

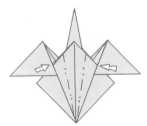

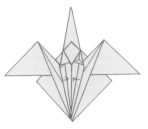

34. Sink to narrow on the left and right.

35. Fold the top edges into the middle and squash triangle.

36. Fold the small edges, revealed in step 35, into the center.

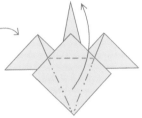

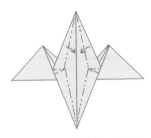

37. Turn over.

38. Petal fold the top flap.

39. Narrow the left and right flaps as in steps 28–30.

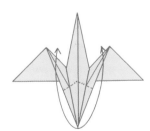

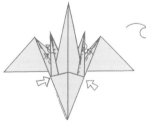

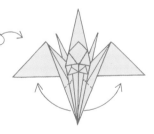

40. Reverse fold the top point from the bottom at the left and right so that the points are a bit inside of the top corner of the wings.

41. Narrow the points by reversing the extra width in, then turn the whole thing over.

42. Reverse fold out the 2 hind legs.

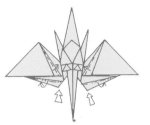 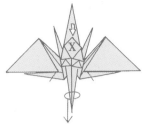 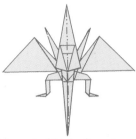

43. Thin out the legs by reversing in the extra width.

44. Reverse fold the legs down, then reverse fold out feet. Pull the tail down spreading point X.

45. Mountain fold the figure in half down the middle and fold the wings up, on a crease right next to the body. There are many layers in the body, so this can be difficult.

46. Reverse fold out front legs and feet. Also, double reverse fold the neck backwards and double crimp out a jaw.

47. Fold the wings loosely along the existing creases. Form head.

48. Completed Long-tailed Dragon.

Cerberus

Cerberus, the fierce three-headed dog, guarded the gates to Tartarus, the underworld kingdom of Hades and Persephone. He kept living mortals from entering and prevented ghosts from escaping.

Robert Lang adds his characteristic detailed touch to this Cerberus model. To create it, he took John Montroll's "dog base" and devised a way of giving it three heads.

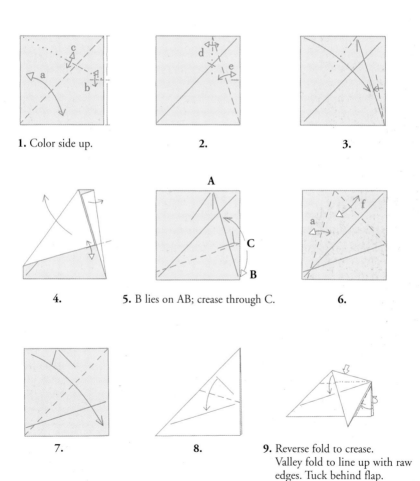

1. Color side up.

2.

3.

4.

5. B lies on AB; crease through C.

6.

7.

8.

9. Reverse fold to crease. Valley fold to line up with raw edges. Tuck behind flap.

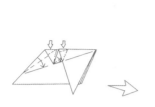

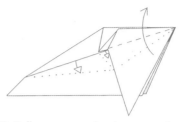

10.

11. Pull out paper and make symmetric. Swing flap up.

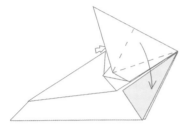

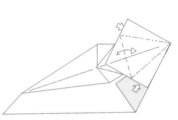

12. Squash fold.

13. Petal fold and unfold.

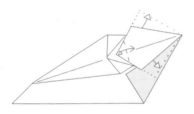

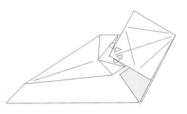

14. Crease, then unfold to 14.

15. Tuck underneath. You have to open out the model to do this.

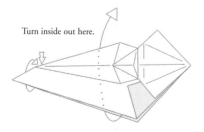

Turn inside out here.

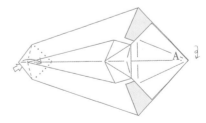

16.

17. Squash fold and turn over.

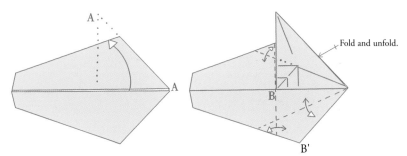

18. Pull point A through as far as possible.

19. B comes to B'.

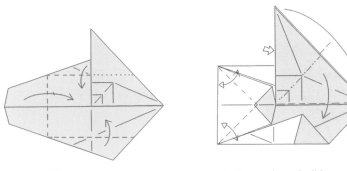

20.

21. Crease through all layers.

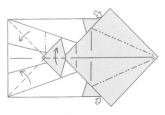

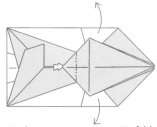

22.

23. Sink on existing creases. Unfold.

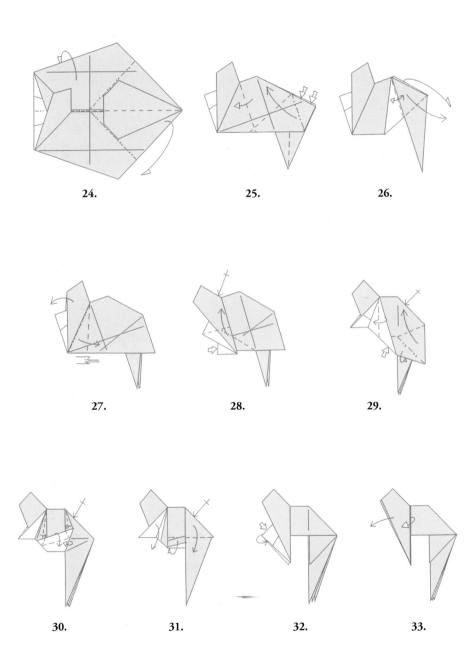

24.

25.

26.

27.

28.

29.

30.

31.

32.

33.

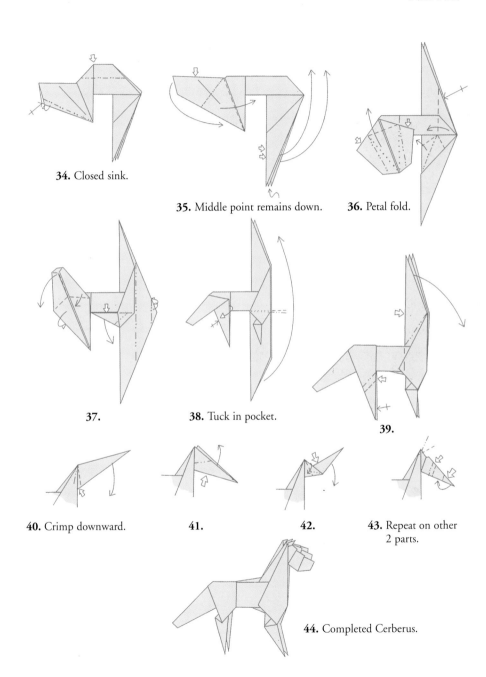

34. Closed sink.

35. Middle point remains down.

36. Petal fold.

37.

38. Tuck in pocket.

39.

40. Crimp downward.

41.

42.

43. Repeat on other 2 parts.

44. Completed Cerberus.

Credits

Catherine Abbot
Napkin Cuffs, *page 17*

Gabriel Alvarez
Daedalus, *page 105*
Pegasus, *page 110*

Jay Ansill
Three-D Greeting Cards, *page 69*

Neal Elias
Centaur, *page 125*

Matthew Green
Long-tailed Dragon, *page 147*

Gay Merrill Gross
Classic Napkin Folds, *page 21*

Jerry Harris
Gargoyle, *page 100*

Mark Kirschenbaum
Rearing Dragon, *page 130*

Michael LaFosse
Paper Bat, *page 162*
Lotus Box, *page 168*

Robert Lang
Shiva, *page 136*
Cerberus, *page 154*

Martha Mitchen
Heart Gift Box, *page 61*

Ligia Montoya
Perching Birds, *page 46*
Tropical Flowers, *page 52*

Robert Neale
Ingenious Letter-Fold, *page 28*
Modular Folds, *page 73*
Ouroboros, *page 88*
Wizard and Witch, *page 91*
Winged Dragon, *page 97*

Aldo Putignano
Picture Frame, *page 40*
Bowl, *page 66*

Samuel Randlett
Chalice, *page 57*

Fred Rohm
Renaissance Shopping Bag, *page 43*

Stephen Weiss
Flapping Dragon, *page 116*
Woodland Elf, *page 120*
Unicorn, *page 142*

About the Author

Jay Ansill has practiced origami since he was a young child. More recently, he has used his work in magazine advertisements, book and CD covers, stage sets, and museum exhibits. He has taught hundreds of classes to children and adults. Jay is also a respected musician and composer with several CDs to his credit. He lives in Bucks County, PA, with his wife and daughter. For more information about the author, please visit his website, www.Jayansill.com.

About the Photographer

Mark Hill is a New York City–based photographer whose work has appeared in the periodicals *Bon Appetit*, the *New York Times Magazine*, and *Metropolitan Home*, among others. In addition, he is the photographer for *The International Spud* (Little, Brown).